Views On Elementary Reading Instruction

Edited by

Thomas C. Barrett
Dale D. Johnson
*University of Wisconsin
at Madison*

INTERNATIONAL READING ASSOCIATION
Newark, Delaware 19711

ira

INTERNATIONAL READING ASSOCIATION

Contents

198707

5. Paraprofessionals

Foreword

The eleven papers presented here on reading in the elementary school are varied in nature, catholic in scope, and currently relevant. The editors note that they were selected from over fifty papers presented on this topic at the 1972 convention of the Association in Detroit. Such a large number of papers is ample testimony to the continued vitality of our concern for improving ways of teaching children to read.

My sincere thanks go to the anonymous members of the committee who aided in a selection process in which the authors of papers also remained anonymous. I would further especially thank Professors Barrett and Johnson for the time and effort they have expended at their own volition in rendering so significant a service to IRA and its members. Among other things, they reviewed the work of the review committee and made important decisions in editing and organizing this group of papers. I heartily recommend the results of their labors to you.

Theodore L. Harris, *President*
International Reading Association
1971-1972

Introduction

The 1972 International Reading Association Convention held in Detroit provided a platform for more than fifty addresses on various aspects of teaching reading in the elementary school. From this number, a board of independent judges selected eleven papers for their fresh insights, practical suggestions, and sound advice, among other attributes. In so doing, the judges have provided the readers of this volume with a cross-section of the many and varied topics on elementary reading discussed at the 1972 Convention. The editors applaud those who were involved in the judging of manuscripts for a difficult job well done and for the often unrecognized efforts they exerted in doing it.

To say that *Views on Elementary Reading Instruction* will provide the reader with all he needs to know about the area would be misleading. The volume does, however, highlight some extremely important and provocative topics by including papers which, to our way of thinking, reflect some of the concerns of the times for those who are involved in the teaching of reading.

The past decade has seen a rising awareness of the special requisites of reading programs for the culturally diverse. Considerable psycholinguistic research evidence has shown the inseparable intertwining of language development and reading acquisition. In Section One Robinson describes eight inferences for reading instruction which he has derived from psycholinguistic and sociolinguistic insights. Two additional papers in this section focus directly on the needs of the culturally diverse. Some unfounded assumptions about "disadvantaged" children are criticized by Bryant, and she suggests needed curricula for innercity children. Rosen describes psycholinguistic reading activities intended for use with the culturally and linguistically diverse. In the final paper of this section, Brunner criticizes three premises about urban school reading instruction.

The language experience approach has piqued the interest of many teachers of reading because of its obvious and subtle possibilities as a medium of instruction. In Section Two the reader may find more fuel for the fire. Shohen, for example, highlights the importance of using a child's thoughts, language, and actions as a basis for teaching him to read. On the other hand, Matteoni presents techniques and activities to use with the language experience approach in order to develop various skills and abilities.

Section Three touches in two ways on the affective dimension of reading, a dimension which needs much attention. First, Schubert emphasizes the importance of using pupils' interests as a means of involving them in reading. Second, Loepp provides a sevenfold plan for individualizing reading instruction and in so doing shows concern for students' interests and attitudes.

With the increasing popularity of the middle school, more reading educators have become interested in the special skills required for content area reading. Two papers which deal with reading in the content areas are included in Section Four. Differences between narrative and expository styles are highlighted by Dulin. He presents a number of interesting suggestions for teaching and evaluating content area reading. Snoddy's paper is a review of selected literature pertaining to the research study skills.

In the final section of the volume, Dauzat focuses on the contributions paraprofessionals can make to a reading program and provides a miniguide for their participation in the classroom.

Many questions about elementary reading remain unanswered. We feel the papers included here suggest some answers and, perhaps more importantly, raise additional questions.

TCB
DDJ

LANGUAGE, READING, AND THE CULTURALLY DIVERSE

1

Based on psycholinguistic and sociolinguistic insights he has gained, Robinson presents eight inferences of importance to teachers of reading.

Psycholinguistics, Sociolinguistics, Reading, and the Classroom Teacher*

H. ALAN ROBINSON
HOFSTRA UNIVERSITY

Many teachers are bewildered and uncertain about concepts, procedures, and materials related to linguistics, psycholinguistics, and sociolinguistics; many are being bombarded by "loud and fuzzy" cries of publishers who announce "linguistic programs, psycholinguistic phonics, and dialectic patterns." Indeed, teachers should be pleased that we are probably learning more about language and the language user today than ever before and that eventually we may have more complete and better organized information available. At this stage, however, the teacher must depend largely on his own ability to digest the information coming toward him at a fast and furious pace. (Not an easy task, to be sure, but an essential one.) There is no, and should be no, linguistic or psycholinguistic or sociolinguistic *method* of teaching reading. All methods of teaching reading involve linguistics (the study of language) in one form or other. And it is as foolish to speak of a psycholinguistic method or sociolinguistic method as it is to speak of a psychological or sociological method of teaching reading.

Any reputable approach to the teaching or learning of reading cannot help but make use of some of the basic tenets

*Sections of this paper have already been published: H. Alan Robinson, "Psycholinguistic Inferences for Reading Instruction," in Vera Southgate (Ed.), *Literacy at All Levels*. London: Ward Lock Educational, 1972.

of linguistics, psychology, and sociology. The amalgamation of the disciplines adds dimensions of vital concern to the teacher and the learner, for the spotlight is focused on societal or group language patterns (sociolinguistics) and the ways individuals think and behave (psycholinguistics) as they make use of language for their various purposes.

Goodman (2) synthesizes much of his thinking (growing out of his research) about psycholinguistics and reading. He states, "As children strive to get meaning by processing written language, they begin to develop comprehension strategies. These are strategies for selecting and using the graphic information, predicting an underlying grammatical structure, and relating their experiences and concepts to written language." He goes on to suggest, "If teachers can understand the significance of what children do as they read, they can provide useful, relevant materials, detect hangups children acquire, help a child to acquire useful strategies, and let go of nonproductive strategies. The teachers will be able to monitor the reading process as it develops."

In light of these introductory comments, let me present some of the insights I have gathered. They are by no means agreed upon by all psychosociolinguists, linguists, or reading experts but have been generated from the oral and written discourse of scholars, as well as from my varied experiences as I have studied these interrelated fields over the past years. Some are broad concepts which would stimulate little or no argument; others are speculative and possibly controversial. The number of inferences stated is by no means inclusive or conclusive; they are limited by both my present thinking and the space allotted for this paper.

1. *The cultural patterns of a group or groups within the classroom should be studied, understood, and respected by the teacher.* Time spent in trying to learn about and understand group behavior patterns will pay off in establishing the kind of group empathy instrumental as a base for enlarging oral communication and beginning or enhancing

students' interactions with written communication. Once a group believes the teacher is honestly attempting to understand and respect aspects of its traditions, goals, and interest, communication lines are opened.

2. *The behaviors of individuals within the classroom should be studied and understood by the teacher.* Granted, doing case studies of the individuals in a classroom is time consuming and often complicated, but the result can be significant. The teacher may want (at first) to conduct a "mini-case study" of those few students who seem to present problems. Case studies applied to one individual often help the teacher as he begins to look at another individual. Gates (1) says that the conducting of comprehensive case studies with learners has transformed many teachers ". . . from routine operators to insightful artists." The result of a case study is bound to help the learner and the teacher understand and respect each other—the basic ingredient of instruction.

3. *The learner's dialect should be understood and respected.* Language is used (normally) to communicate meaning. The student comes to school with a remarkable knowledge of how to gain meaning from oral language. Specifically, he is adept at obtaining meaning from his dialect—that which has been heard and used in the learner's environment prior to school entrance and during school attendance. If the teacher tries to understand and respect that dialect and doesn't deprecate it, the individual will be able to express his thoughts. If the teacher studies the dialect and learns what is part of that dialect system and what is not, the teacher will know when corrections are called for.

If the dialect is denigrated and not understood, the learner will stop using language almost completely in the classroom or will cease to use it for positive communication and will look for ways of using it in negative behavior. In any case, he will most likely make little conscious effort to learn the changes in the rules presented by the dialect used in school and business—often referred to as "standard English."

If the student is given many opportunities to use language

as an expresser of meaning and to search for meaning in the language of others, he will gradually learn to cope with "standard English" which represents a dialect needed at this point in time to gain upward mobility in society. Without doubt, transitions to "standard English usage" must be made or the school is failing in its task.

4. *Initial reading experiences should capitalize on the learner's dialect.* The learner should recognize a need to transfer from oral to written language in order to receive a message of importance. Such an abstract, high-flung goal as "you need to learn to read because it will help you all the way through school and life" is a feeble excuse for reading in the minds of most students. Initial messages to be read should parallel the learner's dialect both semantically (words and groups of words representing understood concepts) and syntactically (language patterns or structures familiar to the language user). There is some question in my mind whether the teacher would want to parallel the dialect graphophonologically (sounds written down as stated). If a child is permitted to use his own dialect when reading orally—for there is no problem when he is reading silently— I see little reason for having to have the orthography printed or written in the dialect. As long as the comprehending is adequate, the pronouncing does not have to be standard.

If the learner writes some words in dialect, that is his prerogative. Certainly there will be times when the teacher will write some phrases in dialect when it is natural to do so in simulating a written conversation. The important point to be made is that the individual must not feel that his dialect is automatically turned off once he approaches the printed word. Indeed, part of the problem in learning to read may result from the tension created by the need to read and write accurately, something that had never been demanded when the child was learning to speak and listen.

5. *Instructional materials and recreational materials used in beginning reading programs should be selected on the bases of significance and relevance.* Reading, particularly in

beginning stages, should (as implied earlier) satisfy immediate goals. The messages should have significance and relevance in terms of solving problems, supplying enjoyment, and enhancing ability. The material read should, inasmuch as is feasible, satisfy the present interests and needs of the specific learners in given learning situations. Too often our reading programs have been largely literature programs emphasizing the literary and the narrative. Certainly part of the reading diet should be narrative in nature, but the diet should be well balanced. In all probability, a large number of boys and even girls would gain more from beginning reading experiences if initial materials placed more stress on expository and utilitarian reading.

The manner in which the material is written should also be considered. Styles and syntactical structures should not, certainly at the outset, be far outside the language experience backgrounds of the learners. In the past many preprimers and primers began with sentence structures and writing styles foreign to the learner. Although perhaps not as rhythmic, "John sees Mary. Mary sees John." is certainly a lot closer to the basic language patterns of most dialects in contrast to "See, John, see. Oh, Mary, see." Readers rather quickly learn to contend with a variety of styles and structures *if* the transition periods are carefully planned.

6. *Since most messages are transmitted through a series of interrelated words, sentences, or paragraphs, minimal attention in reading instruction should be placed on the recognition and analysis of individual, isolated words.* Maximum attention to phonic and structural analysis on individual words isolated from the rest of language is uneconomical and needlessly frustrating for many students. In this type of instruction the learner can depend on only one aspect of language, the graphophonological, rather than make use of the syntactic and semantic as well.

In my opinion, large numbers of students have been prevented from learning how to read and from developing an enjoyment of reading through the use of the word list method. Not only have they come to think of reading as a mechanical exercise but they have been kept from using cues represented within the total context of a message. They have been equipped to decode words rather than language.

In all probability, for some learners in some situations, teachers do have to place emphasis on helping learners figure out grapheme-phomeme relationships. This inference is in no way a denunciation of such help. It is instead a plea for not using just one aspect of language as a tool, particularly on words removed from their natural environments. The inference which follows suggests a strategy for using the many cues to figure out a message represented by written symbols.

7. *The learner develops, and needs to be helped to develop, strategies for unlocking the ideas found on the printed page.* Rather than place attention on absolute accuracy in reading the words in print, emphasis should be placed on utilizing the least number of cues to obtain the author's meaning. As a number of psycholinguists have implied or stated, reading should be an intelligent guessing game, making use of whatever aspects of language are needed as the reader searches for the meaning. The learner should be encouraged to make errors in his search for meaning; this approach is how he learns. The teacher should understand, encourage, and delight in the miscues of his charges as they make use of such a strategy in search of meaning. According to Smith (3) in his recent book, *Understanding Reading*, "This readiness to take chances is a critical matter for beginning readers who may be forced to pay too high a price for making 'errors.' The child who stays silent (who 'misses') rather than risk a 'false alarm' by guessing at a letter or word before he is absolutely sure of it may please his teacher but develop a habit of setting his criterion too high for efficient reading."

The "guessing game" should become less chaotic as learners learn and teachers help in the development of strategies to use when parts of messages are confusing or unknown. The most essential strategy appears to be the utilization of context. The student should learn to search a given context intensively when stopped by a confusing or unknown message. The context which provides the answer may be a phrase, clause, sentence, group of sentences, paragraph, or group of paragraphs. Frequently, the reason for not understanding the message will be an unknown word or two or a new use of known words. An inspection of interrelationships among words and the function of the word or words within the structure of a sentence will often result in the unlocking of the message. Such is the reading behavior of the mature reader, and emphasis should be placed on the use of context strategy right from the very beginning of reading instruction.

When context alone is not sufficient, the reader should be encouraged to use the strategy of looking at the beginning of the word or words. The learner should be helped to relate again this inspection of initial graphemes to the context. These combinations of strategies will frequently permit the reader to interpret the message. (Obviously if the reader keeps meeting words with the same initial graphemes and can't read them, the teacher will develop an assistance lesson interrelating the graphophonological cue with context cues.)

In some cases readers will want and need to inspect the final grapheme in a word or to divide a long word into parts as they try to figure out the word in relation to context. By the time readers resort to this strategy the message either becomes clear rather promptly or they are forced to resort to the help of the dictionary or some other outside authority.

Whatever the strategy or group of strategies learned and employed, the important point to be made is that the teacher should be available to help the learner marshall what he already knows about language and what he is learning into useful procedures for unlocking ideas in print.

8. *Reading tasks are dictated by the nature of the language user, the nature of the material, and the purposes to be met.*

There is no specific sequence of skills to be taught in reading instruction. Sequences of skills to be learned in various reading programs have most frequently been devised on the bases of speech development, developmental needs of children, and/or the logical thinking of program designers. In reality, though, sequence is only relevant when related to the language knowledges and inadequacies of particular learners, the nature of the material to be read, and the purposes for reading. Reading skills are actually a system of strategies the learner acquires for discovering meaning and utilizing it. If the strategies are appropriate for the purpose of the reading and the nature of the material on hand, a given reading task will be successful.

In that light, it behooves a teacher to help the learner diagnose his language strengths and weaknesses in relation to the material to be read. For example, if the reader is beginning to encounter numerous words with the vowel pattern of *ea* within them and is unable to figure them out even with the help of the existing context, the teacher should structure some help. The learner should be given opportunities, using familiar context, to note that the vowel pattern of *ea* is most often pronounced in two ways—ē or ĕ (with flexibility allowed for dialect differences). The student may then go back to the less familiar context and try the new strategy. For those readers who have already generalized the *ea* pattern, there is no need for them to "be taught."

The nature of the material to be used must also be carefully explored, for there is no reason for the learner to attempt to acquire a strategy at a given point in time when it will not be functional. A complete reading program cannot be presented in any meaningful way within the framework of any given set of reading materials. Strategies for unlocking ideas should be acquired as a reader utilizes printed materials throughout a school curriculum. The wide variety of patterns of writing requires a variety of strategies for interpreting them. For example, it might be argued that one strategy a mature reader ought to develop is the ability to note cause and effect relationships in printed material. This strategy can be practiced in some narrative materials, but the cause-effect writing pattern occurs most often in expository materials, particularly in social studies. Here, then, is the most reasonable time and place to learn how to unlock ideas presented in a cause-effect pattern.

Purpose constantly interacts with the reader, the writer, and the material to be read. Any piece of material can be read utilizing different strategies for different purposes, and the task is hardly ever clearcut. For example, if the reader is searching for the solution to a problem, he doesn't care much what the writer's purpose was—as long as the information is available. In all probability, if the writer's purpose and the reader's purpose happen to coincide, the task would be a trifle easier. A very different set of strategies has to be employed, however, when the reader is trying to discover the writer's purpose—particularly if the writing is somewhat subtle.

CONCLUSION

When we look at reading from a psycholinguistic and/or sociolinguistic viewpoint, we became very much aware of the complexities involved in having two people—the reader and the writer—carry on a meaningful dialogue. It becomes evident that more study is needed of the process or processes of reading. But obviously psycholinguistic and sociolinguistic insights exist which can be useful in guiding each learner to strengthen strategies as he unlocks ideas in a variety of materials for multiple purposes.

REFERENCES

1. Gates, Arthur I. "Characteristics of Successful Teaching of Reading," in H. Alan Robinson (Ed.), Reading: Seventy-Five Years of Progress. Supplementary Educational Monographs, No. 26. University of Chicago Press, 1966, 15.
2. Goodman, Kenneth S. "Reading: The Key is in Children's Language," Reading Teacher, 25 (March 1972), 508.
3. Smith, Frank. Understanding Reading. New York: Holt, Rinehart and Winston, 1971, 25.

Although Rosen directs his remarks to teachers of the "disadvantaged," his fourteen reading activities—many quite innovative—could be adopted by all classroom teachers.

Reading and the Disadvantaged: Some Psycholinguistic Applications for the Classroom Teacher

CARL L. ROSEN
KENT STATE UNIVERSITY

". . . Joe is a fourth grader who has been retained once for poor reading. He knows his letters and his sounds but doesn't understand vowels. He reads slowly at the second grade level and is making little progress because he is not trying. He is sullen, has very poor English, and is unwilling to read aloud. Is this a perceptual or neurological problem?"

The preceding remarks are a classroom teacher's description of a disadvantaged child. The teacher also talked of "disordered neighborhood" and of "lack of parental interest." The typical middle-class stereotypes of personality, culture, and language were present in most of her comments. She was troubled. Despite apparent intense efforts to teach this fourth grader more and more about phonics, he seemed to be responding even less. She then referred to Joe's purported awkwardness and his left-handedness, saying, "Doesn't this mean he's *supposed* to have trouble in reading?" Finally, Joe's teacher decided to come up with something which would help alleviate her anxiety in the face of having exhausted the alternative available to her: She generated the "visual perceptual" and "neurological" etiology.

A study of her statement describing Joe's reading and language behavior reveals an orientation to reading that suggests both she and Joe would benefit from her acquiring more modern understandings of the reading process. Indeed, if she were to look into the literature in reading and linguistics of the past five years, she might experience a renewal of excitement, interest, and enthusiasm for the educational aspects of her work.

The classroom teacher is the dominant person in the issue of teaching reading—not the pediatrician, neurologist, optometrist, or school psychologist. Her abilities to recognize, accept, nourish, arouse, and channel the interests, abilities, and needs of her pupils and her facility to create conditions that arouse thought, activity, and imagination among pupils are critical. She generally needs to know more about language, reading, and the children she is responsible for; and she must learn what implications this information has for her classroom teaching. Her children (particularly pupils like Joe) and how they read and behave toward reading are reflections of what she knows and does not know, how she teaches and what she does not teach. A teacher's behavior in the face of learning difficulties with given pupils is a reflection of her professional competency. It is unfortunate when the teacher's attention is diverted needlessly from her major function to areas representing only minute aspects of importance in her work.

From the outset the following points should be made clear: 1) The remarks that follow are not meant to exclude such factors as human physiology in learning or the need for massive changes in our society, including our schools and colleges. This paper will not deal with these issues. 2) The remarks that follow are not intended to be prescriptive, only descriptive, of some teaching options that could be utilized by the classroom teacher. These options illustrate another aspect of the reading process beyond decoding. 3) The activities to be described might be useful as supplements to existing developmental and corrective programs. They might be particulary useful for word-bound or grapheme-phoneme-bound youngsters who deal with reading in an ineffectual and overly piecemeal fashion. 4) The activities to be described here could be useful for pupils who require some different approaches to reading improvement from teachers who are ready to look at the reading process from a new perspective. 5) The activities to be described require exploration, trial, scrutiny, and refinement; they are far from finished products. A brief commentary on language factors will precede the discussion of these instructional activities.

Language and the Disadvantaged Child. Children have internalized most linguistic rules of their language before they come to school. There is no justification for labeling disadvantaged children verbally deficient, with the exception of children with demonstrative sensory, neurological, or affective pathology. Language behavior, however, is subject to variations—both linguistic, as in the case of dialect or bilingualism, and psychocultural, as in the case of the child who can speak but will not do so in school. Whatever factors might underlie language behavior, the child's linguistic system is his medium of communication. It is a precise, predictable, satisfactory, and useful means of interacting with others as far as the child (and linguists) are concerned, regardless of whether it fits his teacher's expectations. It should not be tampered with by the ignorant.

Reading and Schooling. Schooling is almost always an interference with important needs of children. Along with the suppression of interaction, activity, play, expression, and sometimes human dignity, there are inordinate demands made on previously successful language behaviors—particularly in the area of receptive language. The child must become a listener, and this charge requires him to be passive, attentive, and silent. When he does have the opportunity to speak, the culturally diverse child learns quickly that he is "different." The implications become clear to him that being different is not a "good" thing. His teacher might also be unable to separate her misguided belief in the necessity of correcting his "poor English" from her responsibility to teach him to read. She might be unable to properly utilize her district's reading program; or her own instructional biases favoring synthetic word-decoding techniques might dominate her teaching style. Whatever the case might be, the child will experience some confusing introductions to the learning-to-read process.

The successful teacher, however, values people and understands the origin and the nature of language. She is aware of the learner's needs to be regularly reinforced for language behavior and knows that linguistic messages, in both speech and print are interdependent wholes, not independent entities. She knows that because language is cyclical, involving reflection, expression, and reception, it requires active human interaction in a dynamic environment. She knows that the manipulation of ideas in a free and secure learning environment is critical to growth in all language areas including reading.

Following are more than a dozen activities which would, in the writer's opinion, contribute to a teacher's ability to enhance all language abilities of her children, but particularly reading. Space permits only a brief overview of these techniques.

READING ACTIVITIES FOR THE CLASSROOM TEACHER

1. *Active manipulation of print* via multisensory input involves a series of activities of highly motivating and reinforcing nature: a) cutting letters for bulletin board captions; b) printing blocks for newspapers and setting printing type for pupil's original stories to be duplicated; c) sign and poster making; d) typing stories; e) writing invisible ink messages; f) diagram and map making; and g) printing captions for timelines, projects, experiments, scrapbooks, and dioramas.

2. *Action directed approaches* require active and immediate responses to printed messages. These activities focus attention on the information-bearing nature of print

and create opportunities for pupils to eventually produce print by writing their own messages. A wide variety of activities are possible, for example: a) directions on cards, such as, "Open your book to page 12" or "Put your pencil in your desk" or "Let's go out and take a walk"; b) games in print, such as, "Hop on your left leg three times. Do the same on your right one. Sit at my desk"; c) treasure hunt directions, such as, "Find the note under your red book" (the note says), "Find the key on page 22" (note attached to key), "Open the drawer in back of you" (Finds a box with a note), "This Coca Cola is for you!"

3. *Choral reading and impress techniques* imbed patterns of fluent language flow, enhancing understanding of connection between print and spoken language. These techniques require carefully chosen materials and the sensitive selection of children who would profit from frequent exposure to this type of oral reading. The teacher must be a competent diagnostician who, through observation and skills, can identify pupils whose fluency in reading can be enhanced through use of these approaches. The techniques are based upon providing frequent exposure to print via oral reading experiences that are carried out in natural conversation fashion.

4. *Connecting conversation and prose* demonstrates differences between the two modes by systematic contrast and switching in game-like fashion. A pupil may respond orally, dictate to the teacher, or print out responses himself. For example, Teacher: "Hi, Joe, how are you doing?" Joe: "O.K.—I guess." Teacher: "Really?" Joe: "No, lousy I mean!" Contrast the latter with the prose version: "Miss Jones was Joe's sixth grade teacher. She met him in the dentist's office and asked him how he was doing in high school. At first he said 'O.K.,' but then he admitted, 'not so good.' " Having discussions of differences between conversation and prose as well as having pupils write out conversations and then rewrite them into prose would be useful.

5. *Cloze procedures* develop insight into use of language

signals in print and could improve the use of context clues. Passages could be presented utilizing either nth word or nth part of speech deletion. There are possibilities for a child to employ this strategy with other techniques as well, such as language experience stories that he himself dictated or wrote, action-oriented approaches, and cryptography. For example: Bill jumped away as a hail of __1__ came to him. He fired at the place in darkness from which the __2__ came. Suddenly a figure rushed him. He swung his rifle at the __3__ and knocked him down. The pupil would respond from among these multiple choice items: 1 a) arrows, b) bullets, c) rocks, d) bombs; 2 a) shots, b) spots, c) slots, d) stops; 3 a) figure, b) man, c) person, d) lady. In this example sentence interrelationships have an important influence on choices.

6. *Cryptography* requires a high degree of attention to information processing and has strong motivational influence. Pupils could eventually produce their own codes and pass secret messages to one another involving more and more personally developed and elaborated codes. The teacher herself must first develop and demonstrate to pupils simple cryptograms—printed messages in coded form—either by means of new orthography or by imbedding irrelevant and confusing units into message-bearing sentences. The child must break the code and give the message, for example: "Marigold Red is cows dogs the name of cats chickens a dangerous enemy birds pigs spy." (After every third word two plural animate nouns are imbedded.) Pupils would benefit in many areas of reading from this technique. By developing their own graphic symbolization some pupils would be helped to understand the place and use of symbols in messages. Those using standard orthography would have high information-providing experiences, and the technique could provide an interesting modification of the language experience approach.

7. *Grammatical substitutions* sensitize children to grammatical relationships while scanning a message. A pupil

rapidly scans a sentence and indicates his choice, for example, a) side-by-side verb inflections: My sister (has, have) a boyfriend; b) within sentence substitutions: My mother saw a mouse, or My mother sawing a mouse, or My mother saw a mice; c) orally produced cues: John (ask, asks, asked) a question. The pupil should experiment with changes in intonation and stress to deal with sentences such as these. To avoid influence of phonological differences due to dialect, the activity should not be carried out via oral reading.

8. *Prolonged sentence games* develop the ability to string multiple verbal concepts and interrelate them into a major idea, following the technique of "This is the house that Jack built." This approach can also influence pupils' perceptions of spelling patterns.

9. *Vocabulary practice-sorting* provides drill through rearranging stacks of word cards rapidly; the words used should be referentials (symbols for objects, things, places, events).

10. *Scrambled or distorted order of input* requires reconstruction of printed message, sensitizing pupils to information extraction via rapid message recognition and reordering. Consider these examples, a) scrambled words: "Book your close" or "Green was John's bike broken"; b) scrambled syntax: "To walk downtown/it was easier/when the traffic is heavy"; c) jumbled words: "Billiseleven-yearsoldandisinthefifthgradeattheArlingtonSchool."

11. *Semantic substitution* sensitizes a child to variations in use of vocabulary by requiring him to provide verbally or by sorting cards a synonym or antonym for underlined lexical items in sentences. For example, "The *happy* boy was hungry." The choices could be *cheerful, merry, empty, famished.* The child should produce sentences in print for others to manipulate. Specific parts of speech to substitute could be systematically dealt with.

12. *Simple to complex sentences* develops the ability to recognize and expand simple concepts, encourages the use

of prepositions and conjunctions, and provides experience with complex syntactical units in print. Some examples are a) declarative sentences: "The man bought the coat." "He liked it." Expansion: "The man who bought the coat liked it"; b) exclamatory sentence-to-declarative: "Don't touch that." Expansion: "Mary saw the large spider and yelled 'Don't touch that' "; c) interrogative sentence to declarative: "Where did you go last night?" Expansion: "Father asked Bill, 'Where did you go last night?' "

13. *Sentence interrelationships* develop an understanding of how sentences and their interrelations signal meanings. Pupils can produce or search out examples in their texts and from other sources, for example, 1) The man climbed the pole. 2) He fell. 3) His arm was broken. Idea: His arm was broken due to the fall. Through study and manipulation of ideas in sentences and discussion of the relationships, pupils' abilities to extract information from print can be enhanced.

14. *Unit-centered-project approaches* provide "reading-to-learn experiences" as well as experiences for multimedia activities—constructing, drawing, creative writing, etc. Techniques involve heavy use of relevant reading content in information-extracting activities for individual and group projects. These approaches integrate all language skills through group processes and social interaction between pupils through committee work and oral presentations. Study skills, references techniques, and writing and thinking skills are included in the approaches which require a highly competent teacher who is able to guide pupils and help them locate and utilize materials.

CONCLUSIONS

Disadvantaged pupils like Joe require teachers who can break from compulsive teaching patterns and develop conditions for freeing themselves and their children so that language, thought, and natural curiosity are released and applied to learning to read. The active production and manipulation of print in information-generating and extraction experiences in reading, rather than passive and piecemeal computerized word study, should be applied with many pupils like Joe who read as they were taught to—often slowly, tediously, thoughtlessly, and with much pain. The activities presented here are suggestive of some experiences with print that could provide pupils with some of the kinds of practice and experience that will help develop more fluent reading.

The disadvantaged child has been labeled "deficit, different, deprived," and recently, "perceptually" or "neurologically impaired." Rather than applying esoteric labels to individuals or groups who have not been taught effectively, educators should begin concentrating their attention on ways to reeducate themselves and, thus, modernize their approaches to the teaching of reading. The activities listed are designed to develop in children the habit of perceiving that sentences convey meaning and, as units, are far greater than the individual sound or word constituents within. Word-bound and letter-bound poor readers like Joe can profit from activities which will unlock their linguistic resources and allow them to interact meaningfully with printed language.

REFERENCES

1. Bormuth, J. "An Operational Definition of Comprehension Instruction," in K. Goodman and J. Fleming (Eds.), *Psycholinguistics and the Teaching of Reading.* Newark, Delaware: International Reading Association, 1969, 48-60.
2. Chomsky, C. "Reading, Writing, Phonology," *Harvard Educational Review,* 40 (May 1970), 287-309.
3. Chomsky, N. "Phonology and Reading," in H. Levin and J. Williams (Eds.), *Basic Studies on Reading.* New York: Basic Books, 1970, 3-18.
4. Clark, K. "The Cult of Cultural Deprivation: A Complex Social Phenomenon," in G. Natchey (Ed.), *Children With Reading Problems: Classic and Contemporary Issues in Reading Disability.* New York: Basic Books, 1968, 179-189.
5. Cole, M., and J. Bruner. "Cultural Differences and Inferences About Psychological Processes," *American Psychology,* 26 (October 1971), 867-876.

6. Goodman, K. "The Linguistics of Reading," in G. Frost (Ed.), *Issues and Innovations in the Teaching of Reading*. Chicago: Scott, Foresman, 1967, 204-216.
7. Goodman, K. "Words and Morphemes in Reading," in K. Goodman and J. Fleming (Eds.), *Psycholinguistics and the Teaching of Reading*. Newark, Delaware: International Reading Association, 1969, 25-33.
8. Hanna, L., G. Potter, and N. Hagaman. *Unit Teaching in the Elementary School*. New York: Rinehart, 1956.
9. Illich, I. *Celebration of Awareness: A Call For Institutional Revolution*. New York: Anchor Book-Doubleday, 1971.
10. Jongsma, E. *The Cloze Procedure as a Teaching Technique*. Newark, Delaware: International Reading Association, 1971.
11. Kaluger, G., and C. Kolson. *Reading and Learning Disabilities*. Columbus, Ohio: Charles E. Merrill, 1969.
12. Marquardt, W. "Language Interference in Reading," *Reading Teacher*, 18 (December 1964), 214-218.
13. McDavid, R., Jr. "Dialectology and the Teaching of Reading," *Reading Teacher*, 18 (December 1964), 206-213.
14. Rosen, C. "Needed Research in Language and Reading Instructional Problems of Spanish Speaking Children," in J. Figurel (Ed.), *Reading Goals for the Disadvantaged*. Newark, Delaware: International Reading Association, 1970, 278-290.
15. Rosen, C. "Poverty Children and Reading Curriculum Reform: A Broad Perspective," *Educational Technology*, 10 (May 1970), 38-45.
16. Rosen, C., and W. Ames. "An Exploration of the Influence of Dialect on the Oral Reading of Sentences by Black Children, Grades Three through Six," *Reading World*, 11 (March 1972), 201-209.
17. Ruddell, R. "Psycholinguistic Implications for a Systems of Communication Model," in K. Goodman and J. Fleming (Eds.), *Psycholinguistics and the Teaching of Reading*. Newark Delaware: International Reading Association, 1969, 61-78.
18. Seymour, D. "The Differences Between Linguistics and Phonics," in M. Dawson (Compiler), *Teaching Word Recognition Skills*. Newark, Delaware: International Reading Association, 1971, 74-79.
19. Torrey, J. "Illiteracy in the Ghetto," *Harvard Educational Review*, 40 (May 1970), 253-259.
20. Wardhaugh, R. "The Teaching of Phonics and Comprehension: A Linguistic Evaluation," in K. Goodman and J. Fleming (Eds.), *Psycholinguistics and the Teaching of Reading*. Newark, Delaware: International Reading Association, 1969, 79-90.
21. Wiener, M., and W. Cromer. "Reading and Reading Difficulty: A Conceptual Analysis," *Harvard Educational Review*, 37 (Fall 1967), 620-643.

Bryant takes issue with the unfounded assumptions about 'disadvantaged" children and discusses curricula which can meet the needs of the innercity child.

Counteracting the Problem of Negative Stereotyping

WILLA C. BRYANT
LIVINGSTONE COLLEGE

Topics related to the effectiveness of certain methodologies, the quality of research, speed reading, learning modalities, and instruction for the disadvantaged were discussed in the 1965 publication, *Current Issues in Reading.* Findings from research and innovative programs have helped to resolve many of these issues. Yet, some issues remain to plague us, and new issues continue to appear on the scene.

One of the most crucial issues in reading today, brought into focus by the desegregation of faculties and pupils in many public schools, is the inability of black pupils to read efficiently along with the inability of teachers to teach them to read. This situation is viewed as an acute problem by parents and laymen, as well as by educators. In view of the many projects, programs, and procedures that show promise in curing the reading ills of the black and disadvantaged, why do the problems persist? Some writers believe that identification and description of the disadvantaged negate the possibility of their being taught and that the terminology used to describe these students gives rise to negative assumptions.

DESCRIPTIONS AND ASSUMPTIONS

The literature is replete with descriptions of the disadvantaged. Reisman (17), Havighurst (7), and Deutsch (5) make descriptions similar to those of Passow and Elliott (16) who say that the disadvantaged are:

A group characterized by a) language inadequacies, including limited vocabulary and syntactical structure, inability to handle abstract symbols and complex language forms to interpret and communicate; b) perceptual deficiencies, problems of visual imagery and auditory discrimination and spatial organization; c) a mode of expression which is more motorial and concrete than conceptual and idea-symbol focused; d) an orientation of life which seeks gratification in the here and now, rather than in delaying it for future advantage; e) a low self-image, denigrating one's potential as a person and learner; f) too modest aspirations and motivation to achieve academic goals and processes; and g) limited role behavior skills and inadequate or inappropriate adult models.

As a group, they reveal inability to cope with the group demands and expectations of the school program and personnel; accumulative academic retardation and progressively deteriorating achievement pattern; and a high incidence of early school withdrawal.

On the basis of such descriptions Baratz and Baratz (1) point out three assumptions that are made:

1. Upon entering school the black disadvantaged child is unable to learn in standard educational environment.
2. This inability to learn is due to inadequate mothering.
3. The ghetto environment does not provide adequate sensory stimulation for cognitive growth.

THE IMPLICATION OF THE ASSUMPTIONS

For many teachers the preceding assumptions imply that black children are deficient in some way. They possess deficiencies as a result of social pathology and, consequently, suffer so from cultural and economic disadvantages that they cannot be expected to learn as white children do.

Research, however, fails to support these assumptions. Although black children continually fail in our schools and do not benefit from the educational environment, there are no data to substantiate that they are incapable of learning. According to Baratz (2), the inadequate mother hypothesis was created to account for a deficit that does not exist. There is no evidence to support the thesis that the absence of books, newspapers, and magazines in the home, and the fact that mothers seldom read or talk to their children, hinder children's intellectual ability. Neither is there evidence which demonstrates that reading to children is essential for their learning to read or that such reading will enhance their language development. Irwin (10) indicates that children who are systematically read to, babble more; but he does not demonstrate that they are linguistically more proficient than children who are not read to. Research into the ghetto environment reveals that ghetto children, instead of lacking stimulation, are exposed to excessive stimulation.

These assumptions, and the underlying stereotyped thinking, become useful means of categorizing black youngsters and convenient explanations for failure to teach them to read. When teachers' future expectations are based on assumptions that have no validity, teachers contribute significantly to the creation of inefficient readers within the classroom. Many teachers experience a welter of negative feelings when confronted with youngsters who appear different, unmotivated, and unscrubbed. Cuban describes the classroom climate for the disadvantaged as ranging from abrasive to patronizing. Such conditions are in no respect conducive to learning.

Several studies have been conducted to determine what effect on children a teacher's values, beliefs, attitudes, and expectations may have. Studies by Gibson (6), Katz (13), HYOU (9), Kraraceus (14), Reisman (17), and Rosenthal and Jacobson (19) tend to support the thesis that pupils perform in accord with teachers' expectations. In a study designed to validate a type of educational self-fulfilling prophecy, Rist (18) attempted to clarify the basis upon which differential expectations are formed and how they are directly manifested within the classroom. Through his research we have developed both a system for analysis of the factors that are critical in the teacher's development of expectations for various groups of pupils and an understanding of the process by which such expectations influence the classroom experiences for the teacher and the student. The development of expectations regarding an academic potential and capability was traced from the kindergarten teacher on through the various levels. Rist took the position that the first teacher, by a series of subjectively interpreted attributes and characteristics that appeared to be significantly related to social class criteria, divided the class into groups expected to succeed (fast learners) and those expected to fail (slow learners). Differential treatment was accorded to the two groups in the classroom with the fast learners receiving a majority of the teacher's time, attention, and reward-directed behavior. Those designated as slow learners were taught infrequently, subjected to more frequent control-oriented behavior, and received little, if any, supportive behavior from the teacher. The gaps in completion of academic material between the two groups widened as the school year progressed.

A similar process occurred in later years of schooling, but the teacher no longer had to rely on subjectively interpreted data as a basis for ascertaining differences in students. Teachers were able to utilize a variety of informational sources such as past performance, preregistration forms, tentative lists of students on welfare, and a number of other sources. None of the sources of information on which grouping was based was in any way related to academic potential.

THE EFFECTS OF NEGATIVE EXPECTATIONS

This kind of behavior on the part of teachers, indicative of their expectations, reinforces the inequality of education and the humiliation of the pupils. A well-designed program will fail in the hands of teachers who are convinced that the disadvantaged lack such attributes as motivation, self-esteem, social skills, and verbal facility and, therefore, cannot learn. Such attitudes doom the pupils to failure. Implications for the future of children lacking middle-class credentials are tragic. Clark (3) says that the record of public education in the United States historically demonstrates that despite previous conditions of economic or cultural deprivation, human beings have been able to use education as a means of overcoming economic disadvantage. Pupils with social and economic disadvantages are not inherently, nor inevitably, poor students. Schools tend to make them so by assuming and acting as if they were.

COUNTERACTING THE PROBLEMS

An examination of the various compensatory or enrichment programs that have been successful in raising the academic achievement of minority group students reveals that the significant new ingredient invariably is more effective teaching by teachers whose expectations can raise the performance of the pupils.

If we could forget the labels, cast aside the false concept that disadvantaged children cannot learn to read, and concentrate on research that points the way to effective methods and procedures for teaching—methods and procedures that take into consideration the individual's needs, his learning style, his stage of development, and other differences that make him unique—the stage would be set and the environment structured for learning to take place. Provisions should be made for the differing needs of the black child from low socioeconomic environments. Individualized instruction is not new. Over the past ten years there has been an increasing awareness of differences in learning behavior resulting from divergent cultural backgrounds, from personal experiences, and from varying interests and achievement levels.

Research indicates that curricula that counteract the problems associated with the disadvantaged are those based, not on deficits, but on differences and on the newer findings of the behavioral scientists regarding how children learn. These curricula are developmental; and their content is current, sophisticated, and challenging. Loretan and Umans (15) suggest that these newer curricula for the disadvantaged are in direct contrast to early programs that were bland, watered down, and dull. The newer content is not only current and imaginative, but also is content packed.

The methodology encourages the student, through experiences, to develop his own conclusions or generalizations. The student no longer listens passively to what the teacher tells him; he becomes a partner in the learning act. In the newer curriculum the cognition studies of Piaget and others have some implications for the teaching of reading. There is a general understanding that the move is from concrete examples to abstract ideas and that sequentially ordered step-by-step treatment of material helps children progress from literal reading to inferential and evaluative reading. This procedure enables children to meet success more often than failure, thereby reversing the failure cycle. Teachers of the newer curricula are aware of the evidence that some children can process information better through one modality than another. Auditory, visual, and kinesthetic experiences, therefore, are given to help children learn to read. The newer reading curricula are not fixed but are subject to modification intended to fit children. Reason and knowledge are the foundations on which the programs rest. Objectives are being stated in terms of behaviors that can be evaluated. The mastery of word recognition skills is not left to chance.

In addition to refining the skills the children have learned in the primary grades, considerable emphasis is placed on developing skill in reading in the content fields.

The newer programs recognize that the selection of appropriate materials at all levels is crucial for children of divergent backgrounds and experiences. When pupils approach a subject for the first time and find that it is presented in terms and concepts alien to their experiences, they are likely to find the subject matter incoherent and irrelevant. Failure of teachers to recognize this finding has created many of the problems currently besetting American educators. The changing nature of children's materials that are used for reading instruction is evidence of attention to the psychology of learning, which views interest as a stimulator of behavior. Multiethnic textbooks are available—even though they never leave the bookshelves in some schools. Many of these textbooks depict impartially a true picture of all groups. Zimet (20) has developed a guide that can be effectively utilized in organizing and differentiating the program of instruction. Teachers of children from cultures different from the all-white suburban middle-class culture can use this guide to successfully individualize instruction between and within groups.

The use of self-instructional devices and programed materials will help the teacher to pace the lesson so as to hold the interest of both the slowest and the fastest pupils, rather than work on the assumption that all are slow. Instructional units are based on definite behavioral objectives. The learning activities are also based on the objectives and can be varied to allow for different learning styles.

Finally, when teachers cease to act upon assumptions that are not validated, when the view is no longer clouded by labels, and when the findings from research are applied to teaching, we will be well on the way to solving the crucial issues related to the disadvantaged.

"The heart of the reading instructional program is a competent, dedicated teacher who knows both the theory of reading instruction and the ways different children learn." A teacher who accepts the responsibility for student learning recognizes that accountability aids in assuring that the immediate and long-range goals of the students are met. For as Cleland (4) said, "The battle for literacy will be won in the classroom—with the teacher as the foot soldier of the campaign. He is the crucial element in any effective procedures employed in the classroom."

REFERENCES

1. Baratz, Stephen S., and Joan C. Baratz. "Early Childhood Intervention: The Social Science Base of Institutional Racism," *Harvard Educational Review*, 40 (February 1970), 29-47.
2. Baratz, Stephen S., and Joan C. Baratz. "The Social Pathology Model: Historical Bases for Psychology's Denial of the Existence of Negro Culture," APA Paper, Washington, D. C. 1969.
3. Clark, Kenneth B. "Answer for 'Disadvantaged' is Effective Teaching," in Harold Full (Ed.), *Controversy in American Education* (2nd ed.). New York: Macmillan, 1972.
4. Cleland, Donald L. "Education's Moonshot," *Reading Teacher*, November 1971, 136.
5. Deutsch, M. "Minority Groups and Class Status as Related to Social and Personality Factors in Scholastic Achievement," in M. Deutsch, et al (Eds.), *The Disadvantaged Child*. New York: Basic Books, 1967.
6. Gibson, E. J. "Perceptual Learning in Educational Situations," paper for the symposium in the research approach to the learning of school subjects, Cornell University, mimeo, 1966.
7. Havighurst, Robert J., and Bernice L. Neugarten. *Society and Education* (3rd ed.). Boston: Allyn and Bacon, 1967.
8. Holloway, Ruth Love. "Beyond the Ringing Phrase," *Reading Teacher*, November 1971, 118-128.
9. HYOU. *Youth in the Ghetto*. New York: HARYOU, 1964.
10. Irwin, O. C. "Infant Speech: Effect of Systematic Reading Stories," *Journal of Speech and Hearing Research*, March 1960, 187-190.
11. Johnson, Marjorie S., and Roy Kress. "Matching Children and Programs," *Reading Teacher*, 24 (February 1971), 402.
12. Karlin, Robert. *Teaching Elementary Reading*. New York: Harcourt Brace Jovanovich, 1971.
13. Katz, I. "Review of Evidence Relating to Effects of Desegregation on Intellectual Performance of Negroes," *American Psychologist*, 19 (1964), 381-399.
14. Kraraceus, William C. "Reading: Failure and Delinquency," *Today's Education*, October 1971, 53-54.
15. Loretan, Joseph, and Shelley Umans. *Teaching the Disadvantaged*. New York: Teachers College Press, Columbia University, 1966.
16. Passow, A. Harry, and David L. Elliott. *Education in Depressed Areas*. New York: Bureau of Publications, Teachers College, Columbia University, 1963.
17. Riesman, F. *The Culturally Deprived Child*. New York: Harper and Row, 1962.
18. Rist, Ray C. "Student Social Class and Teacher Expectations: The Self-fulfilling Prophecy in Ghetto Education," *Harvard Educational Review*, 40 (August 1970), 411-449.

19. Rosenthal, R., and Lenore Jacobson. *Pygmalion in the Classroom.* New
    York: Holt, Rinehart and Winston, 1968.
20. Zimet, Sara G., et al. *A Teacher's Guide for Selecting Stories of
    Interest to Children.* Detroit: Wayne State University Press, 1968.

Three premises felt to be inherent in reading instruction in urban schools are criticized by Brunner for being unfulfilled, unhelpful, or inaccurate.

Reading and Urban Education: An Analysis of Some Traditional and Emerging Premises

JOSEPH BRUNNER
MONTCLAIR STATE COLLEGE

The major goal of this paper is to raise some questions which are important to consider if we are to counteract some of the most recent trends in reading instruction in urban education. No conscious attempt will be made to separate the "bad" guys from the "good" guys. If grouping and classifications of this type are made, they will be the reader's inferences rather than those of the writer.

As individuals involved in some way with the instructional scheme of schools, we are by definition extensions of the basic assumptions and premises upon which the schools operate. It behooves us, therefore, to examine some of these operational premises and assumptions. After they have been examined, we may discover a set of statements concerning the instructional program of the school with which we do not agree. This so-called "consciousness of discrepancies" is the seed of change itself.

A questioning attitude is urged by the writer.

Before examining some of the propositions surrounding reading instruction, a few words about the nature of the topic are necessary. First, when speaking about the "reading problem of urban children," one must avoid the easy generalizations often derived from newspaper headlines.

Our urban schools obviously have retarded readers, but schools also have "good" readers. In an attempt to measure reading achievement one must keep in mind, furthermore, that the skills measured at the elementary levels may be different from those being measured at the intermediate and secondary levels. Hence, reading competency can only be defined vis-a-vis the measuring instrument at a particular grade level.

Likewise, comparisons between systems employing different tests must be made with caution (6). With these considerations in mind, the writer offers the following analysis of some basic premises around which urban schools are organized.

PREMISE I

Urban schools exist to teach children the three Rs. At first glance this statement appears quite accurate. Upon a closer examination, it becomes increasingly clear that urban schools fail to teach reading to a large segment of the population they serve. In Disadvantaged Children: Health, Nutrition, and School Failure, Birch and Gussow (2) report on Davison's and Greenberg's study to locate an urban slum school where the children have made it. "Making it" was defined as being up to grade level in reading and mathematics. Davison and Greenberg surveyed the records of some 1,300 elementary school children and found only 80 children who met the standard the researchers set—an incredible ratio of success to failure (1 in 16!).

Schools readily admit failure as they report low reading scores. The New York Times of February 20, 1972, contains an article titled "Scribner Asks for Improved Instruction in Reading." Commenting on the continuing decline in the reading scores of New York City children, Chancellor Harvey B. Scribner declared, ". . . we have to accept the fact that the reading problem is very serious in New York City."

But as noted earlier, looking at a city in toto is at best misleading. For example, in the New York Times article it was reported that while some schools reported reading scores two years above the norm, others reported scores two or more years below the norm. In essence, the 1971 test results showed that children going to schools in low income areas (mostly black and Puerto Rican) were once again not being taught to read well enough to achieve higher scores on standardized tests.

Writing in the Harvard Educational Review, Stein (8) depicts this phenomenon as a bimodal curve in reading achievement. "It peaks at two-and-a-half years below grade level, falls to nearly zero at grade level, and then rises to a peak again at two-and-a-half years above grade level." Generally speaking, the reading scores can be viewed as statements of the school's success with mainly middle and upper income white children on the one hand and statements of failure for mainly low income black and Puerto Rican children on the other hand.

Historically, children from low income backgrounds have not been taught the three Rs. For an educational system that advertises "learn more, earn more, stay in school," the economically disadvantaged child who naively comes to school to learn to read sometimes may feel that he does not learn much in school. He leaves for various reasons and often is pushed out. Even if he does remain in school, the economic system is not so lucrative as the slogan suggests, especially if the child is black or Puerto Rican.

The premise that schools in the urban milieu teach children to read can also be challenged when one looks at the nature of the school itself. The urban school is set up to serve the adult who earns his living there. The children are secondary to this purpose; in fact, too often only lip service is paid to educating the children.

PREMISE II

Diagnosis of behaviors in our urban schools is a precursor to worthwhile instruction. Most of us have been exposed to what is considered an educationally sound principle in reading instruction. Although stated in various ways, that principle, in effect, states that we must diagnose our children before any worthwhile program of instruction can begin. The more analytical a particular profile sheet appears on a test, the more we are apt to use that instrument. If that test is not sufficient, we choose one with an even greater and more complex diagnostic profile. In this writer's opinion, the endless search for the perfect instrument is "to dream the impossible dream."

We, as educators, have unfortunately emulated the medical model for diagnosing psychoeducational behaviors. An overview of that model and some of its shortcomings are presented here. Generally speaking, the medical model deals with the following four areas: causation, classification, prognosis, and treatment (3).

A further analysis of these categories in the context of education will demonstrate that the kinds of questions we ask about children and the answers we seek are based on the premise that this model is appropriate for educators. For example, in medicine (humble apologies to the AMA) the causes tend to be either singular or tangible; while in education the causes of reading retardation (if one can believe the experts) are multiple and less tangible. In medicine there exists relative agreement in terms of classifications; however, often within the same school the psychologist, the reading teacher, and the learning disability specialist cannot agree on how to classify a "disability" should one exist.

We also know that when children are diagnosed, the dependent variable in terms of classification and treatment tends to be the person conducting the diagnosis. Stated somewhat differently, the educational training, background, and biases of the examiner are more apt to be written into a report than something objective about the child. Pygmalion not only exists in the classroom but also in the diagnostic setting.

Wolfensberger (10) analyzes the "superstitious beliefs"

surrounding the "sacred cow" (diagnosis) which has been enshrined in some type of mystique. The fact that this has become an esoteric topic can be ascertained when observing a specialist talking to a classroom teacher regarding "poor" Johnny. My own experience dictates that classroom teachers will not ask specialists what a particular term means unless they feel comfortable with the person first. After all, who among us could not pass a vocabulary test on learning disability terminology.

The implications of these realities seriously suggest that classroom teachers as well as specialists in all disciplines be exposed to the historical context from which our current beliefs about testing and treatment of populations have emerged.

In urban schools this examination of beliefs and myths is even more important. Some children who have not had prior experiences in testing situations, or are unaware of the strategies required to "survive" an individual diagnosis, may be labeled "antisocial," "hyperactive," "language deprived," or as one who "does not relate well to the examiner."

This writer feels that contrary to the hopes of some of our educational idealists, there will be a continual thrust in the area of testing in the next decade.

Lest we forget, no matter how much we refine qualitatively our psychometric devices, a major function of schools is still the sorting of children.

PREMISE III

Disadvantaged children who attend our urban schools suffer from social, mental, linguistic, and perceptual deficits which have deleterious effects on the ability to learn. The fact that this "deficit model" of behavior is readily accepted in our schools can easily be confirmed if one looks at the cumulative folders of children attending the urban schools. (Low reading scores are not synonomous with the "deficit model." According to the schools these deficits are a causal factor of low reading ability.)

When the responsibility for learning is placed on the child, as is the case with the "deficit behavioral model," the schools have a built-in rationalization for not teaching the children. An illustrative point is cited to support this "rationalization process" by school personnel. Writing in the *Harvard Educational Review*, Valentine (9) reports on a conversation between a guidance counselor and a parent. The mother had asked the counselor why children in her neighborhood public school so often fail to learn. The counselor replied, "We find that children in our school who don't learn either are brain damaged or don't have a father in their home...."

In the general area of reading instruction, disadvantaged children are often labeled "language deprived" or "linguistically impaired." These categories, aside from yielding little information about the child and how he might be taught, are also specious. A child who does not, or will not, perform in some given language context (school), should not be judged as being unable to perform. He may be competent linguistically, but because of other variables (e.g., the affective environment that he is asked to perform in may lack support) he chooses to remain laconic.

There also exists some evidence which suggests that classroom teachers often make mistakes when talking about their children's language output. Shuy (7) reports on the results of a doctoral dissertation in which the researcher asked a group of urban teachers to identify the language problems of their students. After listening to a tape recording of their children and then characterizing the linguistic problems, Shuy reports that the researcher found a low correlation of response to reality. (Eight percent of the teachers reported their children as having meager or limited vocabularies.)

Once again the labels these teachers used to describe their children reflected deficit assumptions about behavior.

Classroom teachers and reading specialists often point to visual-perceptual problems in urban disadvantaged children as the reason for poor reading ability. This diagnosis assumes one important thing about the nature of visual perception. That is, if disadvantaged urban children who are achieving poorly in reading had improved visual-perceptual functioning (as measured by a test of visual perception), they would show concomitant gains in reading achievement.

The research on visual perception and its relationship to reading improvement does not make this assumption as valid as some would like to believe. Commenting on "perceptual-motor activities in the treatment of severe reading disability," Balow (1) states:

> Surprisingly, in numerous searches of the literature by this author. . .no experimental study. . .has been found that demonstrates special effectiveness for any of the physical, motor, or perceptual programs claimed to be useful in the prevention or correction of reading. . . .

Yet Balow recommends the inclusion of such programs in the primary grade curriculum.

In the *Journal of Learning Disabilities*, Cohen (4) interprets the visual-perceptual deficit in terms of reading instruction. He reports that his clinic records ". . . did not show any differences in the treatment success rate between retarded reading children with perceptual deficits and those without." What does seem likely to be effective is a well-planned instructional program in certain reading skills.

It seems to this writer that beyond a minimal level, the ability to read is not a function of perceptual competency as is often stressed.

SUMMARY AND CONCLUSIONS

This paper analyzes some widely held premises regarding the education of our urban children. By no stretch of the imagination have all of the "traditional wisdoms" which go into making decisions in our urban schools been discussed. Other areas of concern which should be scrutinized in urban education are:

1. The validity of current evaluation models in judging the effectiveness of urban reading programs.
2. The validity of our assumptions regarding the sociological and linguistic homogeneity of urban ethnic groups.

Only when these assumptions and others are analyzed and questioned can our urban schools offer a pluralistic approach to teaching and evaluation. In reading instruction, for example, the concept of pluralism could result in a substantial reduction in the number of children being labeled "retarded readers."

Finally, the role of the reading teacher in our urban institutions should be that of reconstructing the urban milieu (if it is devastating to the child) and not remediating the child's behavior to fit this devastating environment.

REFERENCES

1. Balow, Bruce. "Perceptual-motor Activities in the Treatment of Severe Reading Disability," *Reading Teacher*, 24 (March 1971), 513-525.
2. Birch, Herbert, and Joan Dye Gussow. *Disadvantaged Children: Health, Nutrition, and School Failure.* New York: Harcourt, Brace and World, 1970.
3. Clarizo, Harvey F., and George F. McCoy. *Behavior Disorders in School-Aged Children.* Scranton, Pennsylvania: Chandler Publishing, 1970.
4. Cohen, S. Alan. "Studies in Visual Perception and Reading in Disadvantaged Children," *Journal of Learning Disabilities*, 2 (October 1969), 498-503.
5. Dentler, Robert. "A Critique of Education Projects in Community Action Programs," in Robert Dentler, Bernard Macklen, and Mary Ellen Warshauer (Eds.), *The Urban Rs: Race Relations as the Problem in Urban Education.* New York: Praeger, 1967, 158-174.
6. Millman, J., and J. Lindlof. "The Comparability of Fifth Grade Norms of the California, Iowa, and Metropolitan Achievement Tests," *Journal of Educational Measurement*, 1 (December 1964), 135-137.

7. Shuy, Roger. "A Linguistic Background for Developing Beginning Reading Materials for Black Children," in Joan C. Baratz and Roger W. Shuy (Eds.), *Teaching Black Children To Read.* Washington, D. C.: Center for Applied Linguistics, 1969, 117-137.

8. Stein, Annie. "Strategies of Failure," *Harvard Educational Review,* 41 (May 1971), 158-204.

9. Valentine, Charles. "Deficit, Difference, and Bicultural Models of Afro-American Behavior," *Harvard Educational Review,* 41 (May 1971), 137-157.

10. Wolfensberger, Wolf. "Diagnosis Diagnosed," in Reginald L. Jones (Ed.), *Problems and Issues in the Education of Exceptional Children.* Boston: Houghton Mifflin, 1971, 63-72.

USING THE
LANGUAGE
EXPERIENCE
APPROACH 2

Shohen highlights the importance of using a child's thought, language, and action as a basis for teaching him to read.

A Language Experience Approach to Reading Instruction

SAM SHOHEN
ROSLYN, NEW YORK,
PUBLIC SCHOOLS

While children grow and develop, they learn to speak as they interact with their environments. Through their senses—hearing, seeing, smelling, touching, tasting—they respond to the world and learn to say the words that label their experiences by copying the words used by people around them.

Usually, no special efforts are made to teach children how to speak. It just seems to happen. Parents and teachers become concerned only when a child seems to deviate radically from the norm and his speech development lags significantly. Fortunately, such a child is in the minority because the vast majority of children learn to speak with little difficulty.

Most children also learn how to read; yet the adults in their lives seem to become overly concerned and involved in the process of teaching them how. As a result, dozens of approaches to teaching reading have been developed and teachers have vigorously sought the "best" way. Through this vigor, however, the importance of learning how to read has been distorted well out of proportion, and countless children have been "turned off" to the joys reading can bring. Why, then, can't children be allowed to learn how to read as they learned how to speak?

IS THERE A BEST WAY?

More has been written about teaching reading than any other aspect of the curriculum. Reading research concludes, however, that there is no best way of teaching reading; and, ideally, a teacher should select the approach that meets the child's style of learning. Although these conclusions make sense, effective objective instruments for measuring learning style still have not been developed. Perhaps in the distant future, learning style will be reported by instruments similar to those now used to measure heartbeat, body temperature, and blood pressure. Until that time, a teacher of beginning readers can capitalize on the natural development of spoken language to allow children to learn to read in a similarly natural way, through a language experience approach.

THE TEACHER AS FACILITATOR

In a language experience approach the teacher allows the child to learn how to read; she serves as a facilitator. She structures a dynamic environment for the beginning reader where he actively interacts by seeing, hearing, tasting, touching, and smelling. She facilitates his realization that his thoughts and actions can be put into spoken words; words that can be written and be read back. Allen (1) says it as a child would: "What I can think about, I can talk about. What I can say, I can write (or someone can write for me). What I can write, I can read. I can read what others write for me to read."

CLASSROOM ENVIRONMENT

In order to teach a first grader to read through his thoughts, language, and actions, the classroom must be alive with things to do, things to think about, things to talk about, things to write about, and things to read. The room should look like an extension of a kindergarten and contain a block corner, a science table, a math table, and a place for miscellaneous materials. There should be pictures, experience charts, messages from the teacher, stories by children who already can write, and various objets d'art created by members of the group. Other things, such as bookshelves filled to capacity, a workshop bench, an easel, tropical fish, gerbils, and hamsters, should be in evidence. In essence, the room should be filled with manipulative and visual materials that titillate the senses.

In a stimulating environment of this nature, children should be given opportunities to move, to look, to touch, to hear, to talk, to choose, and to explore their feelings. Yet, there must be a structure and a routine. Rules and regulations, established by the teacher and the children, set limits and establish a sense of security. Above all, the teacher must spend much time in planning the learning activities that she will facilitate.

A premise of the language experience approach is that experience stimulates thought; thought stimulates spoken words; spoken words can be transformed into written words; and written words can be read if the preceding components are there. A provocative classroom evokes thought, but a child has many other sources of ideas. Stauffer (2) suggests that ". . . every classroom, school building, and playground represents literally an acre of diamonds of ideas." Along with the additional experiences children bring with them to school, it becomes readily apparent that acres of "interest" diamonds are available through personal, home, neighborhood, community, and school experiences.

The teacher cannot always supply first-hand experiences for her children, so she must provide opportunities for them to broaden thought and language through vicarious experiences. Pictures from books, newspapers and magazines, motion pictures, filmstrips, slides, television, records, and tapes are sources for such experiences.

In his book, The Language-Experience Approach to the Teaching of Reading, Stauffer (2) gives examples of actual experience stories dictated by children to illustrate the unlimited resources the teacher can capitalize on. From the personal area—the world of *I, me, my,* and *mine*—Stauffer reproduces children's stories with these titles: "All About Me," "Myself," "Me," and "I Come and I See." There are stories based on home situations: "My Mother," "My Father," "My Baby Brothers," and "My House." From the neighborhood and community come such stories as "My Street," "Where I Live," and "Trip to the Firehouse." Current and seasonal events and school and the curriculum stimulated entries such as "The Easter Bunny," "Spring," "Valentine's Day," "The Pumpkin," "Dental Health Week," "Hatching Chickens," "A Magnifying Glass," "Our Flag," "The Intercom," "Seeds," "My Project," and "Bicycle Safety." And finally Stauffer presents stories dealing with imagination, dreams, and wishes: "What I Want to Be," "A One-Time Magic Garden," "My Favorite Dream," and "The Pirates."

INITIAL STEPS

Having provided the environment and an awareness of the reservoirs for ideas, the teacher must allow children to realize what reading is in a meaningful, matter-of-fact manner. As she proceeds, she will need to emphasize the message-getting, meaning-seeking function of reading. She will not be concerned with vocabulary control or sentence length because the language she capitalizes on is the language of her own children, most of whom have mastered the syntax of English and have amassed a speaking vocabulary of at least 7,500 words by the time they reached first grade.

The steps the teacher will need to follow are essentially the same whether she works with the entire class, a small group, or an individual child:

1. She will have the children focus on some stimulus, whether it be the class pet gerbil or an idea such as "What makes you happy?"
2. By asking questions, she will elicit spoken reactions about the stimulus.

3. She will act as a secretary and record the spoken reactions in written form.
4. She will have the written record read back, immediately supplying the words that have been "forgotten."
5. She will develop a system for retaining the written copy because the first story plus the second story plus the third, and so on, becomes a "basic reading book."
6. She will provide additional opportunities for pupil contact with the written copy.
7. She will help children develop a "word bank" (2) (e.g., words children "know" from their dictated stories that are recorded either on cards or in an alphabetically arranged "word bank book").

SIGHT WORDS AND WORD UNLOCKING

As the quantity of class, group, and individually dictated stories increases, each child should develop a fund of words he recognizes on sight. This fund will serve as a foundation which will enable him to delve into the written ideas of others. Preprimers and primers should be introduced as independent reading experiences for some children or directed-reading-thinking activities for others. The fund of sight words will also serve as a basis for developing independent word-unlocking techniques. The teacher can utilize the words in her children's "word banks" to teach phonics and structural analysis. And since she should be emphasizing reading as a message-getting process, she can highlight the use of context clues as a major word-unlocking approach. For example, children can learn to apply the suggestion: "If you don't know a word, read the rest of the sentence and see if the other words can help you recognize it." Since children can learn how to read as they learned how to speak, those who are exposed to a reading-for-meaning emphasis such as this will develop most of their own decoding strategies.

48   *Using the Language Expreience Approach*

UNLIMITED POSSIBILITIES

The directions the reading program takes from this point can be unlimited. A discussion of these possibilities goes beyond the limited space allowed for this paper. It should be obvious, however, that the language experience approach allows the teacher to be eclectic. She can continue in any direction she desires. If a basal reader is needed by certain children, it can be used. If a more structured phonics program is required by other children, it can be adopted. If a certain youngster loves to write stories himself and thrills at reading them to others, he should be encouraged. There can be a place for individual, group, and entire class reading. The possibilities are endless.

HELP FROM OTHERS

The teacher should also capitalize on every opportunity to secure help from others. She should find people who can come into her classroom to share ideas, to take dictation, to hear children read, or to make a ditto of someone's story. These helpers can be parents, older children, the custodian, or even the principal. Everyone can help. A master's degree in how to teach reading is not a prerequisite.

CONCLUSION

Finally, it has to be reemphasized that, when developing a language experience program, the teacher must serve as a facilitator. By utilizing a child's thought, language, and action as a basis for allowing him to learn to read as he learned to speak, she can virtually facilitate success. She must view "failure" as a nonexistent word for her pupils.

REFERENCES
1. Allen, Roach Van. "How a Language Experience Program Works," in Althea Beery et al. (Eds.), *Elementary Reading Instruction: Selected Materials.* Boston: Allyn and Bacon, 1969.
2. Stauffer, Russell G. *The Language Experience Approach to the Teaching of Reading.* New York: Harper and Row, 1970, 37-54, 60-75.

Matteoni presents techniques and activities to use with the language experience approach in order to help children develop knowledge of the mechanics of reading and the ability to decode words, apply thinking-comprehension skills, and use study skills.

Developing Reading Ability Through the Language Experience Approach

LOUISE MATTEONI
BROOKLYN COLLEGE
CITY UNIVERSITY OF
NEW YORK

The language experience approach to teaching reading, by definition, is dependent upon two things: the language of the child and the experience of the child. As such, the approach relies on no published material for initial reading instruction because the scope and sequence of skills needed arise from the specific language experience of the child.

Theoretically, the language experience approach requires that reading instruction and reading material be developed on an individualized basis since language and experiences are unique to each individual. Realistically, however, it may not be possible for the teacher to plan time for the individual contacts which are necessary to implement such a program in a class of twenty-five to thirty beginning readers. Remember, five hours a week would be needed to permit a teacher to work individually with each child in a class of thirty for just ten minutes a week. Thus, if there are no teacher aides or paraprofessionals available, the teacher may find it particularly difficult to structure meaningful independent activities for children with short attention spans and limited repertoires of social and technical skills so that she can be free to work with others individually.

It is possible, however, for the teacher to structure

activities or experiences in which groups or an entire class may participate. In this way experience charts may be developed and used as reading materials. The teacher, using her skill in questioning, may elicit charts to illustrate virtually any reading skill she wishes. It would be misleading to suggest that the reading procedure would rely on a haphazard accumulation of reading charts developed without direction since the teacher controls the learning situation.

Before discussing the development of reading ability through the language experience approach, perhaps it would be best to establish some type of hierarchical order of the subabilities involved. Although any such order would by no means be invariant, it would be founded on native language ability. Beyond this, reading ability is dependent upon a knowledge of the mechanics of reading, the ability to decode words, the ability to apply thinking-comprehension skills to written text, and the ability to use study skills for the acquisition of knowledge and information. The discussion that follows deals with these subabilities and the ways in which the language experience approach relates to them. For the most part, the techniques and activities to be discussed are cast in the framework of one teacher working with one child. Frameworks can, however, be adapted to groups of children.

MECHANICS OF READING

In dictating and subsequently "reading" the chart with the teacher, the child learns that words which are represented by sounds are also represented by symbols. Certain symbols tend to be used over and over, others less frequently. Symbols are ordered on a line from left to right in an established sequence. A thought is introduced usually with a tall symbol and terminated by a dot. Lines of symbols start at the top of the chalkboard or chart and continue downward. When there is a pause in the enunciation of a word, there is a space between the series of symbols. This development assumes that the child has not been introduced to reading in preschool experiences, but it can be adapted to the background the child brings to the reading experience.

THINKING-COMPREHENSION SKILLS

As the child continues dictating and "reading" charts, thinking skills are used as a natural activity and in a natural format. These are the same skills which are classified as reading comprehension skills in traditional reading programs. Of all approaches to reading, perhaps the language experience approach alone requires the reader to develop, use, and reinforce skills such as identifying the topic, stating the main idea and related details, establishing sequence, drawing conclusions, and so on through speaking and listening prior to applying these same skills to printed text.

In dictating a chart, the child is led by the teacher to state the topic. The child then determines what he wants to say about the topic he has selected (the main idea). As he adds information, he is led to discriminate between relevant and irrelevant details. The teacher helps the child stick to the topic by recalling with him the correct sequence in which the experiences occurred. Skills such as drawing conclusions and predicting outcomes form part of the exploratory discussion prior to dictating the chart and may be extracted from the chart through questions.

Skills in critical evaluation are employed when the child discusses with the teacher the quality, completeness, or accuracy of a presentation through such questions as: What do you think might make the story easier to understand? Does this chart give enough information to someone who wants to try your experiment? Did you tell the story as it really happened? Other leading questions may center about the best way of telling a funny experience or the best way of establishing suspense.

DECODING WORDS

As a child develops several reading charts, as they are read back to him, or as he reads them with the teacher, he begins to note several things about the written symbols. When the same word is spoken over and over again, it is represented each time by the same symbols. This pattern indicates that symbols are not sequenced arbitrarily but do follow a pattern which is understood by those initiated into the representational method. If the chart is individual, the child will see the word *I* frequently and will learn to recognize it. If the child has a group chart, the most common word will be *We*. At this point the child will be using configuration clues since word analysis has not yet been started.

As chart development proceeds, the child notes that certain words, such as *me, my, our, the, in, to, was, is, have, they, mother, school, teacher,* and *class,* are used over and over again. From the maze of symbols presented in charts, certain patterns emerge and are recognized. The teacher does not stand by idly waiting for this development; being fully cognizant of words most frequently used in children's books, she directs the child's attention to selected words. For example, after developing the following chart on the chalkboard

> A storm is coming.
> The clouds look like dirty cotton.
> The sky is as dark as night.
> We saw a flash of lightning.
> It's scary.

the teacher may print the word *look* on one side of the chart and say, "This is the word *look;* find it in the chart and frame it." She proceeds in the same manner with *is, the, like, as, we, saw, a, and, of,* or as many of these words as are reasonable for the ability of the child. Through this activity, she is leading a child through a visual discrimination exercise, using words which will be needed by the reader in subsequent experiences.

Any number of activities may be developed from these charts to call attention to and reinforce sight vocabulary in meaningful contexts. The need to ascertain the child's understanding of the words is minimized since these words have emerged from his listening/speaking experiences.

In working with a group the teacher may wish to duplicate and distribute charts for continued use. A chart may be used for visual discrimination of words for some children without the ability to read while, for others, it may be used for the identification of words which are in the sight vocabulary.

Charts can also be used for teaching the sound/symbol relationships of selected phonic elements. For example, after the previously cited chart has been developed and with an awareness of words used in other charts, the teacher might well decide that the child has sufficient resources to be led through the steps of learning the sound/symbol relationship of the initial consonant /l/. The teacher would recall with the child some of the words such as *look*, *like*, *lightning*, and other similar words used in previous charts. Stressing the /l/ sound without distorting it, she would call attention to the similarity in the sound at the beginning of the word.

After the child has indicated, by selecting from among several words, the word or words which have the /l/ sound and by supplying words with the same phonic element, the teacher may then lead him through the auditory-visual association of the phoneme with the grapheme. Being careful to keep the initial letters aligned, she would elicit from the child words with the phonic element and list them on the chalkboard. Through questioning, she would call the child's attention to the letter so that he could isolate this letter from all other letters in the words as being common to all the words. It is not necessary to elaborate further here on the method of teaching phonics. A method was illustrated in order to show the resources available for teaching this important reading skill.

Similarly structural items for study may be garnered from a chart or charts. A sufficient number of progressive and past verb endings, possessives, contractions, compounds, and multisyllabic words among other structural items appear which may be used for teaching a particular element.

STUDY SKILLS

Study skills such as skimming, classification, alphabetizing, following instructions, and so on may be developed and reinforced through the language experience approach. The nature of the experience will determine whether a chart might take the form of a how-to-do-it classification in steps or a two-part classification of properties of elements (magnetic and nonmagnetic), rather than the form of a prose account. Skimming is used constantly as the reader looks for a word, a phrase, or a sentence in answer to a question. If a child is encouraged to keep a word file of the words he can read, he learns to use alphabetical sequence in a functional situation.

CONCLUDING REMARKS

The materials for teaching a good portion of the decoding and comprehension skills in reading are present in charts or stories developed through the language experience approach. The young reader is informally and inductively exposed to these skills. Directed and preplanned instruction is possible. The teacher is the central agent for this instruction, as in most reading programs; however, the teacher has a greater responsibility in the language experience approach because skills are not laid out in sequential order. The teacher selects skills from the charts or stories. This procedure implies a great deal of flexibility. In addition, it is up to the teacher to decide whether a particular skill should be introduced or reinforced. The alternative chosen will determine the type of experience to be structured and the expected chart or story to be elicited. There are several resources listing suggested skills in hierarchical order which the teacher may want to use as a checklist. An excellent resource book, *Teacher's Resource Book for Language*

Experiences in Reading, Levels I, II, and III, by Allen and Allen, has been published by the Encyclopedia Britannica.

If there is a strong correlation between listening/speaking and reading, as has been stated, if the teacher is to capitalize upon children's backgrounds, experiences, and interests in the initial structuring of the learning environment, and if learning theory states that one new variable should be introduced at a time, then the language experience approach approximates a sound method for developing learning ability for all children but especially for those who do not fit the implied characteristics of many published programs.

AFFECT AND INDIVIDUALIZATION 3

Schubert emphasizes the importance of using pupils' interests as a means of involving them in their reading and provides a number of practical suggestions for ways of achieving this goal.

The Role of Interest and Motivation in the Reading Process

DELWYN G. SCHUBERT
CALIFORNIA STATE
COLLEGE AT LOS ANGELES

Interests are motivating forces that channel attention and energize action. One pupil stated, "When I read something I'm really interested in, someone could shoot off a gun in the room and I don't think I would know it." Another said, "Sure, this manual's got a lot of words I dont' know, but that's not going to stop me. I've got to pass that driver's test." The good teacher of reading is alert to the interests of his pupils and enlists these interests to stimulate reading. One teacher had difficulty with a boy who drew pictures when he should have been reading. Instead of reprimanding him, she showed one of his drawings to the class and said, "Doesn't Jim draw beautifully? Wouldn't it be nice if he drew a picture that told us about this next story?" The boy was delighted and agreed to accept the assignment. But before he could draw the right picture, he found that he had to read the story for complete understanding. Needless to say, receiving recognition for his drawing skills resulted in Jim's improvement in reading.

Ideally, a pupil should be motivated by a basic desire to learn. This drive occurs when he sees reading as a means of achieving desirable and attainable personal and educational goals. When reading provides him with information relating to his interests and gives him answers to questions that concern him, motivating forces are generated. Teachers who wish to capitalize on pupil interests will find interest inventories of great value. As early as 1939, Witty and Kopel (4) published interest inventories for both elementary and secondary school pupils. These early inventories included many aspects of living and adjustment other than activities relating to reading. Some of the questions were answerable with a yes or no while others called for more detailed responses. Although a number of years have passed since these inventories made their appearance, teachers will be surprised to find that the majority of items are as relevant and valid today as they were in the late 30s.

Interest inventories and questionnaires can be found in many professional books, such as those by Bond and Tinker (1), Harris (2), and Strang (3). After looking over several inventories, many teachers feel prompted to evolve their own so as to have questions that are suited to the pupils in their classrooms. The writer recommends this practice. He has seen several excellent teacher-made inventories.

One teacher reported that she needed "a motivation pill" for her classes. Unfortunately, it is doubtful that a capsulated solution to the problem of motivation can be found. Motivation, like reading disability, is an individual matter. An incentive that is successful with one pupil may fail with another. Similarly, a technique or device that works well when tried by Teacher X may not succeed when employed by Teacher Y. Although there are no panaceas, the following items provide some practical suggestions and guidelines for interesting pupils in the reading process.

1. *Capitalize on the law of effect.* The law of effect is inextricably related to motivation. When a child can see value in what he is reading, it is conducive to an increased desire to read. When materials are chosen to broaden or coincide with his needs and interests, a child is likely to accept reading as something worthwhile. "Here," he says to himself, "is what I want to know more about because I can use it." As a forceful and convincing way of emphasizing the value of reading, have fathers who are firemen, policemen, doctors, or lawyers come to the classroom and talk about "ways in which reading has helped me in my work."

2. *Recognize that success and increased competence in reading are motivating forces.* In this connection, teachers should make sure that reading the materials is not too difficult and that goals are attainable. It should be noted that test scores are likely to coincide with frustration levels of reading rather than independent or instructional levels. Teachers should also see that selections are not too lengthy since few poor readers have had the satisfaction of completing a book or story on their own.

3. *Take advantage of social motivation.* A pupil's behavior is greatly influenced by social motives. These can be used to good advantage by the alert teacher. For example, book clubs can be formed to stimulate reading interest. Such clubs can be scheduled to meet during the school day or after school. They can be devoted to reviewing books, to dramatizing books, or to holding book fairs.

4. *Provide students with a knowledge of results.* Since pupils like to know to what degree they are successful, progress charts of different types should be used. Charts can be kept by the students to provide dramatic evidence of progress in the number of books read, vocabulary growth, and rate of comprehension. Since competition with oneself is more effective than group competition, particularly with disabled readers, it may not be desirable to post progress charts. If a child knows from past experience that he has little or no chance to excel, he not only will fail to exert himself but he may develop an attitude of hopelessness and a deep sense of inferiority.

5. *Realize that the personality of the teacher can motivate pupils.* Nothing can, or ever will, supplant the magical power of a teacher who:
   a. Is genuinely interested in children.
   b. Is warm, understanding, patient, and enthusiastic.
   c. Demonstrates by what he does and says that he is confident the children are capable of improving.
   d. Speaks encouragingly to them and reacts positively to what they have done. (A poor reading teacher is

more inclined to be negative in his reaction, often scolding pupils and deprecating what they have done. Praise and encouragement are particularly valuable in building a child's self-concept which often is related to reading progress.)

e. Maintains a mentally hygienic atmosphere in the classroom by having a cooperative democratic attitude, by showing kindliness and consideration for individuals, by encouraging humor, and by showing an interest in pupils' problems.

6. *Employ reading games to provide practice in a way that is purposeful, enjoyable, and conducive to continued learning.*

a. Encourage pupils to help in the construction of the games.

b. Allow pupils to evolve the rules of particular games.

c. Allow pupils to determine the purposes for which particular games can be used.

d. Design games that cultivate self-competition rather than group competition. (But should the games be of the latter variety, they should incorporate a chance element so that poor readers have an opportunity to win in competition.)

e. Encourage pupils to be good winners and understanding losers.

f. Have pupils play those games which help develop skills they need to learn or have reinforced.

7. *Use stimulating questions to motivate pupils' reading.* These questions should be designed to help the pupil project himself into, and identify himself with, the characters in a story. In this connection, it is a safe rule not to ask a question you can answer yourself. Questions should be asked in such a way that the child must answer them in terms of his own experiences, beliefs, and aspirations. For example, instead of asking, "What is the color of Susan's hat?" say, "Why would or wouldn't you like a hat the color of Susan's?"

8. *Give daily opportunities for fun reading.*

a. Provide classroom libraries that contain a variety of books in terms of interest and difficulty level. Make the library center as inviting and attractive as possible. If pupils do their reading in pleasant surroundings, the conditioning that results is positive and beneficial to the reading process.

b. Display books invitingly and enticingly on large, low tables. Provide chairs of the proper size so that children can seat themselves when relaxing with a good book. When books are displayed on shelves, it is advisable to work out a classification and labeling system to make the array of books appear less formidable to the prospective reader.

c. Capitalize on the special motivational appeal of paperbacks. Paperbacks are not only inexpensive, but unlike hardcover books, are not associated as readily with study, examinations, and other unpleasantness. Because of their size and composition, they can easily be slipped into a purse or pocket for ready accessibility whenever reading opportunities present themselves.

d. Encourage your administrator to set aside a room for students which can serve as a free reading lounge. This lounge should provide an atmosphere conducive to free reading. Heavy carpets and pads, pillows for back rests, revolving paperback racks, and a small radio will help to create such an atmosphere.

9. *Employ book reporting procedures that are designed to stimulate reading interest.*

a. Have artistic pupils design book jackets or posters that advertise the books read. Some students may wish to highlight several incidents of a story pictorially so that the book report becomes a picture book. Other students may wish to model clay figures or dress dolls in costumes which depict characters in a story.

b. Encourage pupils to present informal dramatizations of books. The use of colored or painted masks (paper bags may be used) adds realism to children's depictions of the characters in a book or story.

c. Have pupils who write well send a letter to the author in care of the publisher telling how much they enjoyed the book. Invariably, a reply will come which may be posted so that children who see the letter will be prompted to read the author's books.

10. *Issue colorful certificates for book reading.* These can bear the names of the recipients and may be signed by the teacher and/or the school principal. Different colored ribbons or seals may be used to designate levels of merit.

Suggestions such as the foregoing can be helpful in stimulating pupils to achieve one of the most important objectives of any reading program: a lifelong desire to read widely and voraciously.

REFERENCES

1. Bond, Guy, and Miles Tinker. *Reading Difficulties: Their Diagnosis and Correction* (2nd ed.). New York: Appleton-Century-Crofts, 1967.
2. Harris, Albert, *How to Increase Reading Ability* (5th ed.). New York: David McKay, 1970.
3. Strang, Ruth. *Diagnostic Teaching of Reading* (2nd ed.). New York: McGraw-Hill, 1969.
4. Witty, Paul, and David Kopel. *Reading and the Educative Process.* Boston: Ginn, 1939.

Loepp provides insights into and suggestions about individualizing reading instruction through a helpful sevenfold plan.

Individualizing Reading Instruction

KATHLYN V. LOEPP
FORGAN, OKLAHOMA,
PUBLIC SCHOOLS

Each child is unique, like fingerprints. Within this brief statement is the challenge that all teachers of reading must meet during the next decade if the goals of the "Right to Read" are to be achieved.

How can we as educators meet this challenge? Although there may not be a simple solution—a panacea—an individualized approach to teaching reading may be a step in the right direction. Individualized reading is, in fact, more than an approach; it is a philosophy that respects the needs of the individual and highlights the motivational force of his interests. It may not be easy to implement an individualized reading program, but any teacher with the courage of her convictions can do it. The sevenfold plan that follows may be helpful.

INITIATING AN INDIVIDUALIZED READING PROGRAM

To begin, consult with your local school board, superintendent, principal, and reading supervisor. Be aware of the organizational structure of your particular school situation but convince the necessary people of the basic need for an individualized reading program and how it relates to the ongoing program. Before and beyond this action the initiator must consider the importance of 1) well-defined goals and purposes, 2) careful and cooperative organizational planning and scheduling, 3) one's belief in the ultimate benefits that can be derived by this type of instruction, 4) superhuman energy, and 5) an inexhaustible knowledge of children's literature. Above all, one must have the patience of Job.

Several others suggestions are worth noting here. Be content to start your program on a small scale. Be content to build from scratch and suffer through the agonies of scheduling, testing for placement, obtaining of adequate supplies, and the myriad of other obstacles which seem destined to deter one's initial enthusiasm. Breathe often this little prayer:

God grant me the serenity to accept things I cannot change,
Courage to change things I can,
And wisdom to know the difference.

OBTAINING READING MATERIALS AND SUPPLIES

Teachers who individualize a reading program must procure as large a variety of books and reading-related supplies as possible. Proponents of individualized reading have made recommendations as to the minimum number of books needed for each child; however, this number will vary and will depend upon the availability of money, city or county libraries, traveling bookmobiles, or clubs who would furnish books.

It should be borne in mind that the children's needs and interests play a prominent part in the selection and variety of books. Future presidents, lawyers, doctors, construction workers, astronauts, scientists, and teachers are sitting in our classrooms; and provisions and inspirations must be available to meet and support their vital interests. In addition, we must provide materials with a range of readability levels that span the variance of abilities commonly found in a heterogeneous group of children.

Books alone are not sufficient to do the job. Other written materials, including magazines, newspapers, programed materials, and workbooks must be available. In addition, provisions should be made for the use of such modern multimedia educational materials as tape recorders, viewmasters, audio-enrichment materials, sound filmstrips, educational records, movies, educational TV, videotapes, pacers, speed readers, tachistoscopes, overhead projectors, art supplies, easels, and scrap materials. Finally, reading games, either teacher-made or commercial, which facilitate learning of various skills, have a vital role to play in such a program.

THE ENVIRONMENT FOR INDIVIDUALIZED READING

A prime requisite for effective individualization is a flexible arrangement within the classroom for various centers of interest. The rigid "row upon row" of the past must give way to the "push and pull" for instant interest grouping.

A first consideration should be given to an attractive library area where students may browse freely. Open shelves, inviting magazine displays, and colorful bulletin boards featuring outstanding books are all necessary ingredients in encouraging good reading habits.

A skills area gives the teacher an opportunity to work with students individually on any phase of work for which the child indicates a need. A good skills area will have an abundance of workbooks, multilevel kits, special plastic sheets, and grease pencils and a well-organized box of mimeographed phonics materials categorizing the various skills into both sequence and ability levels. Within such a classroom organization, an individualized spelling approach also builds skills effectively. This program can be color coded to represent the different levels, and teacher prepared tapes can give individual students the opportunity to self-pace their own progress.

Single concept tapes, either teacher prepared or commercial, can be placed in a particular area to accompany various lessons. This arrangement gives the teacher the opportunity to pull up a chair and give one-to-one instruction while other students are working independently.

An enrichment center may accommodate the aesthetic

needs of students. Located within this area could be such materials as filmstrips, viewmasters, tapes, educational records, read-along books, picture books, and children's encyclopedias for special interest topics. In addition, an art center would give the manually gifted students a chance at self-expression; a collection of scrap materials could be used for creative projects, puppetry, or illustrated stories.

Finally, a speed center which could extend and improve the visual perceptiveness of developmental and accelerated students should be available. A word of caution at this point is that speed has a tendency to frustrate the remedial reader, so it is a technique to be used with much consideration.

In general, then, organize the classroom in such a way that the child can locate materials readily. Have a method of checking out books and materials that is understood by all. Provide for maximum working conditions with a minimum of confusion. Skilled management on the part of the teacher will be needed or chaos could reign.

ACCEPT THE CHILD WHERE HE IS

The key to individualized reading instruction is diagnosis. A teacher must know a child's weaknesses and strengths and use this information to promote greater independence on the part of the child through teacher guidance and evaluation. Such an approach can promote greater rapport between teacher and student.

Many techniques can be used for diagnosis. Each teacher probably has favorite tests and evaluation techniques for this purpose; some can and should be informal, but some should be standardized. Cumulative folder data and interest inventories can also provide useful information for diagnostic purposes. But once the diagnostic data have been accumulated and evaluated, be prepared to accept what the child is able to give in the way of performance, keep alert to his progress, and let him know that his best is expected.

ORAL READING

Through   the   use   of   the   master   console   and   other electronically equipped listening stations, a unique approach to oral reading has been developed quite successfully. Using such an approach, one teacher can conduct the oral reading activities of an entire class.

The master console, on the one hand, gives the teacher an opportunity to have a one-to-one relationship with as many students as she has individual carrels. Before her she will have the array of books the students have chosen to read. By turning the correct controls, she can monitor, talk back and forth with each student, record his efforts, and present immediate play-back for him to evaluate. This particular one-to-one learning situation has great potential for students who most need individual help.

On the other hand, the more independent students can work simultaneously at other carrels equipped with a program source and headsets. Their responsibility will usually be to complete a developmental task outlined by the teacher. To do this assignment, they may record a portion of the day's reading lesson on tape and monitor it for purposes of self-appraisal. The teacher can also monitor the tape and evaluate the child's reading. Through this procedure students are made aware of correct diction, phrasing, regressions, tonal qualities, and other finer techniques of good oral reading. The electronic age has entered the reading field in a big way, and the results can be particularly gratifying.

KEEPING RECORDS

An individualized reading program would not be adequate without accurate, daily records. The method a teacher chooses for keeping such records is strictly personal. However records are made, they should keep track of such items as skills developed, sight words learned, weaknesses and strengths noted, testing data used (both formal and informal), anecdotes entered as to classroom attitudes and behavior, titles of books read, and conferences held.

It is equally important that the student be taught to keep

his own progress records. Student records might include contracts made in accordance with teacher expectations or charts of the various accomplishments and progress at the respective centers. Records might also include the progress being made toward goals sought by students themselves. Certainly it is important for teachers to share with their students the academic and behavioral objectives set, but it is equally important to stress that they, as students, seek improvement.

THE PUPIL-TEACHER CONFERENCE

The highlight of the program is reached when the pupil and the teacher sit down together to discuss what has been learned. It is also during these shared moments that skills can be taught, weaknesses can be discovered and corrected, future work can be planned, and goals can be accomplished. Most importantly, a lasting bond may be established between a student and a teacher as a result of the rapport developed during conference time.

Not to be overlooked in discussing conferences is the value of holding regular ones with parents. Many schools use this evaluation method in lieu of a formal report to parents. It can be a rich, rewarding experience if adults can sit down and discuss intelligently their mutual concern—the child.

SUMMARY

As stated at the outset, each child is unique, like fingerprints. The challenge which confronts all teachers is whether they can provide instruction that will meet the needs and highlight the interests of each unique being. It has been the theme of this paper that individualizing reading instruction may be a starting point for a breakthrough in meeting this challenge. The criteria for judging its success or that of any other proposal, for that matter, must ultimately be related to the ways the individual meets the complex demands of his world and whether he meets them with dignity and concern for others.

READING IN THE CONTENT AREAS 4

Dulin succinctly differentiates between narrative and expository writing styles. His suggestions for teaching and evaluating content area reading could be usefully adopted throughout the elementary grades.

Teaching and Evaluating Reading in the Content Areas

KENNETH L. DULIN
UNIVERSITY OF
WISCONSIN AT MADISON

Generally speaking, most reading authorities feel that a total, all-school reading program should have at least four major components. Though the precise labels used to identify these parts may differ from program to program, overall they usually come out like this:

1. a developmental reading program
2. a recreational reading program
3. an enrichment reading program
4. a functional reading program

In developmental reading activities, the child learns his basic skills of reading; in recreational reading he applies these skills in following up personal interests; in enrichment reading he gains personal insights through reading; and in functional reading he uses reading as a means of acquiring knowledge. In short, then, we could probably define these four program parts as 1) learning to read, 2) reading for personal enjoyment, 3) reading for personal growth, and 4) reading to learn, with "content area" reading, the topic of this paper, fitting quite clearly into the fourth category, functional reading.

The Need for Instruction in Content Area Reading

The foregoing definitions, however, recognize only the differences in goals among the four types of reading—that is, *why* the reader reads in each of the four situations. A more important distinction, particularly for the teacher, is in the types of materials used.

Developmental reading takes place primarily in specially prepared instructional materials, carefully designed to insure a smooth progression from skill to skill and from level to level. Peopled with school-age characters, laced with humor and interesting dialogue, and accompanied by well-done, multicolor illustrations, such material is generally inviting and fun for children to read. In a sense, then, such material often almost teaches itself.

Recreational and enrichment reading usually take place in supplementary trade books designed by experts with a great deal of care taken to allow for children's interests, abilities, and maturational patterns. In addition, such reading matter is often self-selected. In consequence, then, this material also practically teaches itself.

Functional reading, however, or "content area" reading as it will be referred to in the remainder of this paper, knows no bounds. Textbooks, library reference materials, magazines, and newspapers all fall into this category. And for most of these materials, far less editorial control exists.

It is more important, however, that teachers distinguish among the basic styles of writing used in the four areas: the first three types of material are primarily narrative, while those in the fourth are primarily expository. And this difference is why direct teaching is so necessary in content area reading.

THE NATURE OF NARRATIVE

In a word, narrative materials are "story" materials: short stories, novels, poems, and plays. As such, they are relatively easy to read; they follow a clear story line, a step-by-step plot development, and a purpose-problem-solution sort of sequence. Plotted graphically, they all come out looking much like Figure 1. The story builds and builds; the reader is drawn along by dropped clues, catchy phrases, and figurative language; and finally the boy gets the girl, the good guys win the war, or man triumphs over nature and it's all over.

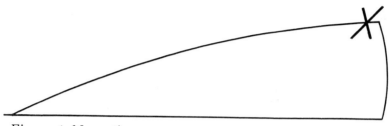

Figure 1. Narrative

Figure 2. Exposition

THE NATURE OF EXPOSITION

Expository writing, however, is developed more like a series of waves, with each wave representing a paragraph embodying a main idea and a set of supporting details and with the brackets above them representing subsection, section, chapter, and unit organization. Though both styles of expression arrive ultimately at the same place—the development of a cohesive set of ideas—each takes a different route. Helping students to distinguish between these two routes is the essence of teaching content area reading. Because these distinctions are so important, let us look carefully at the two in contrast.

NARRATIVE AND EXPOSITORY MATERIALS COMPARED

Narrative and expository materials differ in at least twelve characteristic ways, each of them important to the teacher who faces the task of helping children bridge the gap between the two. These twelve differences are listed below, paired by number from style to style:

Narrative Style	*Expository Style*
1. catchy titles, usually employing personal reference and action verbs, and sometimes even dialogue and/or humor	1. label-type titles, usually in topical form rather than phrased in sentences
2. compelling topics usually related either to the reader's background of experience or life fantasy	2. abstract, generalized topics; rarely light or amusing; usually not directly related to the reader's background of experience or personal interests
3. a sequential "boy gets girl" or purpose-problem-solution order of plot development	3. a deductive, general-to-specifics, order of presentation
4. an imaginative storyline, with dropped hints, tantalizing clues, and figurative language often used to heighten reader interest	4. a heavy-handed "imbedded outline" organizational pattern, with boldfaced headings, subheadings, and cue words used to move from point to point
5. many concrete details, or "word pictures"	5. a great deal of abstraction, with more concern for scholarly accuracy than for ease of reading or compelling description
6. personalized, humanistic characters, often of the same age as the reader	6. relatively impersonal adult characters (if any at all)
7. a great deal of dialogue, sometimes even containing slang	7. little dialogue but if present, often stilted and formal
8. much personal reference, with many proper nouns and personal pronouns	8. little personal reference, with many subordinate conjunctions and relative and impersonal pronouns
9. short, simple, and compound sentences containing many action verbs	9. long complex and compound-complex sentences with many linking verbs
10. a relatively controlled general vocabulary, with new words	10. a technical vocabulary with "old" words often used to

carefully introduced by context and/or pictures	carry new, specialized meanings
11. many esthetically attractive illustrations, often in color	11. black and white charts, tables, and graphs
12. relatively large print and a relatively "light" appearing format and general physical appearance.	12. relatively small print and a "heavy" appearing format and physical appearance

Other differences could be cited, too, such as the settings in which students characteristically make use of each style, the personal feelings with which they approach each, and so on. But these twelve comparisons alone should make the point: content-area reading is clearly different, and every teacher must consciously plan for teaching it if children are to become successful, well-rounded readers.

IMPLICATIONS FOR INSTRUCTION

Several things come immediately to mind when one examines the foregoing lists. Content area reading clearly presents a good many more challenges, both to the teacher and to the student, than are characteristically found in the other types of reading.

1. *Motivation.* To begin with, the motivating of students to read content material almost always demands more work on the part of the teacher than does motivating them to read narrative. And since this material usually has less intrinsic appeal to young readers, a teacher must consciously articulate compelling purposes for reading if students are going to be willing to enter wholeheartedly into it. Purpose-setting questions, advance organizers, and highly relevant, personalized oral introductions to each assignment can be of great help; but, clearly, a "Let's read this next chapter and then I'll test you on it" approach will not do.

2. *Experiential background.* Overall, the most effective way of motivating a group of uninterested readers is to somehow build their own experiential background to the point where they are truly ready to read a selection for good meaning. As William James once said, "We learn best that

about which we already know a great deal." And since the purpose of content area reading experiences is to extend a reader's background of experience into areas about which he knows *little*, this background-building step is absolutely imperative. Stories, anecdotes, audiovisual aids, and personal experiences such as field trips can be helpful, but so can individual student experiences.

3. *Vocabulary.* As noted, the vocabulary used in content area reading materials is not "controlled" as it is in basal readers; rather, it is intentionally utilized to extend background. Thus, every introductory presentation of a selection should include a meaningful introduction of important new words—in context, with a keen eye to the structural elements within words, and with provision made for some oral-aural use of the new words.

4. *Organizational patterns.* Next, since the most striking differences between "regular" reading instructional materials and content reading materials are in terms of writing style, these differences must be noted consciously and made clear to the students. Some of the best ways to do this task are by paragraph study, by pointing out where and when transitional devices are used, and by drawing attention to the use of boldface headings, cue words such as *first, next,* and *also,* and introductory or concluding paragraphs.

5. *Special skills.* Beyond these general characteristics of content area materials, however, certain specific reading tasks remain—timelines, graphs, charts, maps, tables—and specific instruction must be provided as needed on how to use each device. A good part of the time, such teaching can be incorporated into the general introduction to a selection, but sometimes—such as when timelines are first encountered, for example—actual practice sessions may be called for.

6. *Readability levels.* Finally, despite the effective use of all practices, some materials still remain too difficult for certain members of the class. Even at the elementary school level, the middle 80 percent of a class will ordinarily vary as

much as six to eight grade levels in general reading ability, and this range must be considered. Thus, group reading assignments should almost always provide for some sort of differentiation in the difficulty level of the material to be read: "advanced" level materials for the better readers, "lower" versions for the poorer readers, and "regular" materials for the middle half. Sometimes these divisions can be arranged easily, if an abundance of multilevel materials exist on the topic being taught, and at other times it may be more difficult. Either way, some provision must be made for differences by providing a range of materials, by drastically modifying the assignments for different members of the class, or by doing both.

Other points could undoubtedly be made—the importance of consciously teaching good reference skills and of framing good discussion questions following each reading experience—but the foregoing six points are the crucial ones; therefore, they will make up the basis of the following guidelines.

GUIDELINES FOR EVALUATION

1. Does the teacher make conscious provision for motivating students to read the content area materials being presented? And do these motivating techniques aim for intrinsic motivation without employing threats and admonitions about future tests and grades?

2. Is a conscious effort being made to link the nature and content of the reading material to the experiential background of the reader? And do these efforts employ the best available possibilities through media or varied methodology?

3. Is there evidence of conscious concern over the introduction of new vocabulary? Does this introduction employ the best available methodological steps?

4. Does the teacher consciously point out organizational patterns, stylistic devices, format clues, and other aids as they occur in the reading selection? Does he stress in ad-

dition the broad applicability of these aids for future selections?

5. Does the teacher consciously provide for reinforcement and refinement of the special reading skills needed in the content area under study? And are practice materials provided as needed?

6. Are conscious provisions made to allow for individual differences in general reading ability? And are these differences reflected in the nature and scope of the assignments being made?

7. Finally, are conscious attempts being made to regularly teach and reinforce the general skills of nonfiction, expository reading, and study? Does the teacher take advantage of every opportunity to capitalize upon the reading skill resources of each selection used?

CONCLUSION

It may have been noted that each of the listed guidelines contains some form of the adjective "conscious." This was not an idle attempt at parallel structure but rather a "conscious" stressing of the key point of this entire paper: *conscious* consideration for good methodology is what is needed in the teaching of content area reading, and we must accept nothing less.

Snoddy reviews the research efforts of four doctoral candidates whose dissertation research dealt with the study skills. The conclusions are disappointing but provocative.

Improving Study Skills: A Review of Selected Research

JAMES E. SNODDY
MICHIGAN STATE
UNIVERSITY

From 1965 to 1971 at the University of Illinois four doctoral dissertations were designed to investigate aspects of organizing and teaching a selected group of study skills referred to as "research study skills." These dissertations were conducted under the direction of J. Harlan Shores. In addition to directing the doctoral research, Shores conducted ongoing research in the research study skills during the six-year period. His work received financial support from Grolier and from the U.S. Office of Education. Grolier also supported aspects of the doctoral studies. It is the intent of this paper to summarize the thrust, the findings, and the conclusions of this research; to place it in juxtaposition with current practice in study skills teaching in elementary education; and to suggest recommendations for further research and for practice.

The basic thrust of the study skills research at the University of Illinois is stated succinctly by Shores [5]:

> With new knowledge in nearly every field of human endeavor accumulating at an unprecedented rate, it is at once apparent that only a minute fraction of man's total knowledge can ever be taught. If this untaught knowledge is not to be lost to the cultural heritage, and if man's need for this knowledge is to be met, a greater burden than ever before is placed upon the student's ability to learn independently. It is essential then that students master the skills essential to the location, organi-

zation, and use of content that cannot be taught in the public schools and universities. Mastery of the basic skills must have a high priority in public supported education.

The location of information in printed sources constitutes a cluster of basic skills, and this cluster of skills is the "content" of the Illinois research.

REVIEW OF SELECTED RESEARCH

During the 1965-1966 school year, Shores conducted the initial study in the series (5), the primary purpose of which was to develop and try out a plan of instruction in selected basic study skills. These were termed the "research study skills." He also hoped to demonstrate the value of planned teaching of study skills as opposed to incidental instruction and to offer guidelines for the improvement of instruction. The research design attempted to contrast learnings in the study skills under three sets of controlled conditions: ample learning materials and planned instruction, ample learning materials and incidental instruction, and regular classroom materials and no specific study skills instruction. He reported the findings of the study in great detail based on standardized and researcher-made paper and pencil tests; generally, the differences among the three groups in gain scores from pre- to post-tests were not significant. Shores' conclusions (5) drawn from the study, however, include the following significant statements:

1. The success of a study skills program depends largely upon a firm commitment to move the skills into the central stream of the curriculum.
2. Emphasis should be given the study skills in the reading-language arts program throughout the intermediate grades, with opportunity for practice in the content fields, especially social studies.
3. Supplements to textual materials and an adequate school library are crucial to a complete study skills program.
4. There is a paucity of practice materials for the study skills program.

During the same school year (1965-1966) as the Shore study, and using the same pupil sample, Rodgers conducted a study (2) which investigated some of the ways by which measures of selected study skills are interrelated and how study skills measures are related to measures of general achievement, mental ability, and selected reading abilities. Data were obtained by administering seven standardized tests and one researcher-made test designed especially for the study. Item analysis was employed to rearrange all test items under the five basic study skills clusters defined for the study: dictionary skills; library skills; reference skills; map reading skills; and graph, chart, and table-reading skills. Generally, Rodgers found that measures of the selected study skills are positively intercorrelated and that each of the skills is positively correlated with measures of specific and general achievement, general mental ability, and selected reading and general reading abilities. Rodgers also reported a number of positive relationships among the more specific study skills measures.

The 1966-1967 phase of the research included the doctoral dissertation written by Snoddy. It is reported in various sources (4, 7, 8). The focus of this study was the development and trial of a planned, sequential program in selected study skills, designed to be implemented over an approximate time span of one school year. Teaching and directed practice consumed an average of approximately one hour per week over the school year. Results from pre-post testing using standardized achievement tests indicate that, generally, able students who are involved in a planned study skills program can make grade equivalent score gains of well over one year. Approximately one hundred instructional outcomes were compiled for the study (7). These were employed as a basis for the instructional program and were found to be useful. A recommendation which seems to hold promise for improving instruction in the study skills came from the testing program of this study. While it was not used as such, the item analysis grouping of items from all tests into clusters of items measuring each skill area might have proved useful for diagnostic purposes. It might be assumed that the use of accurate diagnostic data for each pupil might have effected more efficient instruction.

Stinson's research was conducted during the 1968-1969 school year. Her purpose was to ". . . develop a reading program which placed greater emphasis on the research study skills, to put the program into effect at the sixth grade level, and to determine the effectiveness of the program" (9). The control group was a sixth grade class that was involved in a "traditional" or basal reading program. The experimental group had a reading program, developed by the researcher, which placed greater emphasis on the research study skills than did the basal reading program. Based on pre-post testing results using standardized achievement tests, Stinson reported the following: 1) The experimental (study skills) program seemed to be neither superior nor inferior to the control group with regard to reading comprehension and vocabulary and 2) the experimental group gain scores exceeded the control group gain scores in every study skill cluster. Some gain score differences were statistically significant; others were not.

During the 1969-1970 school year, Nold's doctoral dissertation took the next logical step by developing and implementing a study skills program which was geared to students who had exhibited deficient achievement in selected study skills (1). A short diagnostic test of selected study skills was employed as a pretest. Nold reported that "The use of the short diagnostic test . . . demonstrated the feasibility of this technique. It greatly reduces the time and effort to collect pretest data necessary for instructional decisions." He used all scores below the median score on the pretest as a means of identifying deficiency but later concluded this method was too arbitrary. He indicated that it did not allow for the student who may not have known one small part of the target skill. Consequently, he recommended that needed research include the investigation of a

research study skills program that would match an individual's diagnosis with appropriate instruction for every
subskill.

Nold also indicated that instruction in those skills that had
been given earlier attention in the primary grades, such as
dictionary skills, had seemed most beneficial. He concluded
that this finding supported the theory that the research study
skills are best developed by a sequential program from first
through twelfth grades.

The diagnostic test used by Nold was the Research Study
Skills Test, Form A, which was developed by Shores and
Newland. Shores' most recent work in the study skills
focused on assessment, particularly on diagnosis. This study
was supported by a grant from the U.S. Office of Education
and is described in Shores' report to that office (3).
Essentially, Shores set out to develop and establish relia-
bility norms for two forms of a short forty-five-minute diagnostic test for grades four, five, and six in the following five
areas: library use, dictionary use, use of references, reading
graphs and tables, reading maps. He was also interested in
the development of five thirty-minute diagnostic tests to be
used to confirm diagnosis in each skill area measured by the
more extensive test.

While Shores believes the diagnostic instruments he
developed need more revision and refinement, a number of
his recommendations are noteworthy. He suggests that the
diagnostic program alone is of little value without methods
and materials to effect improvement following diagnosis. He
recommends   a   five-step   program   of   diagnosis   and
remediation:

1. Administration of the general diagnostic test and in-
    terpretation of the results.
2. Administration of follow-up tests as deemed essential
    within the time to be devoted to these skills.
3. Instruction in areas of weakness.
4. Retesting with an alternative form of the general diagnostic
    test and interpretation of the results.

5. Retesting with an alternative form of the appropriate follow-up tests if it is deemed essential.

In summary, the research reported in this paper offers evidence to support the following conclusions.
1. Measures of study skills are positively interrelated.
2. Selected study skills yield to systematic instruction.
3. There is a paucity of teaching and practice materials for study skills programs; yet short, relatively, simple, materials are extremely helpful in teaching the skills.
4. A systematic study skills program can be implemented at the middle grade level without retarding development of reading comprehension and vocabulary.
5. A study skills program which centers on individual students' weaknesses seems most efficient and productive.
6. The need in study skills programing seems twofold:
   a. Continued refinement of assessment instruments is needed and
   b. teaching and practice materials development is also needed.

CURRENT PRACTICE AND FURTHER NEEDS

While there is little research which concentrates on the status of current practice in study skills teaching, the five writers cited in this paper describe current practice in less than glowing terms. Each of the four cited dissertations refers to numerous leaders in the field of reading who describe a lack of emphasis on the study skills in school curricula. While the selected study skills described here may receive some attention in one or more curricular areas, the skills are seldom seen as central to any area. For example, materials on dictionary skills, library skills, and reference skills are often found in basal reading programs; commercially packaged materials on map and globe skills are available; and chart, table, and graph reading are a part of many elementary mathematics series. Yet these skills are often seen as less than crucial by the authors of children's materials and by classroom teachers.

Shores' diagnosis and remediation recommendation cited offers promise for improvement of instruction of selected study skills. His program would allow the skills to be assembled into a single

program and would provide for efficient instruction based on diagnosis. If such a recommendation were incorporated into one or
more commercial programs, a more widespread teaching of sound
study skills would occur. While it would be desirable if the study
skills were given systematic attention from the primary grades
through secondary school, this procedure does not occur at this
time. However, as Shores states, "Hopefully, when the entire
program is completed, these often neglected research study skills
will find a more secure place in the elementary school curriculum" (3).

REFERENCES

1. Nold, Jack T. "Teaching Research Study Skills in Fifth Grade,"
   unpublished doctoral dissertation, University of Illinois at Urbana,
   1971.
2. Rodgers, Frederick A. "Basic Study Skills as Related to Each Other and
   to General Achievement, Mental Ability, and Reading Abilities in
   Grade Six," unpublished doctoral dissertation, University of Illinois at
   Urbana, 1966.
3. Shores, J. Harlan. *Development of Diagnostic Instruments for Research
   Study Skills in Grades 4, 5, and 6.* Urbana, Illinois: Final Report to the
   U.S. Department of Health, Education, and Welfare, 1970.
4. Shores, J. Harlan, and James E. Snoddy. "Organizing and Teaching the
   Research Study Skills in the Elementary School," *Elementary English*,
   48 (October 1971), 648-652.
5. Shores, J. Harlan. *Teaching the Research Study Skills, Phase I.* Urbana,
   Illinois: Report to Grolier, 1967.
6. Shores, J. Harlan. *Teaching the Research Study Skills, Phase II.* Urbana, Illinois: Report to Grolier, 1967.
7. Snoddy, James E. "Teaching Research Study Skills in Grade Six,"
   unpublished doctoral dissertation, University of Illinois at Urbana,
   1967.
8. Snoddy, James E., and J. Harlan Shores. "Teaching the Research Study
   Skills," in J. Allen Figurel (Ed.), *Reading and Realism*, 1968
   Proceedings, Volume 13, Part 1. Newark, Delaware: International
   Reading Association, 1969.
9. Stinson, Lillian Powers. "Teaching a Reading-Study Skills Program at
   the Sixth Grade Level," unpublished doctoral dissertation, University
   of Illinois at Urbana, 1970.

PARAPROFESSIONALS 5

Dauzat suggests twelve specific ways paraprofessionals can contribute to the reading program in cooperation with and under the supervision of the reading teacher.

Wise Utilization of Human Resources: The Paraprofessional in the Reading Program

SAM V. DAUZAT
LOUISIANA TECH
UNIVERSITY

The era of ecology has dawned, generating intense concern for the wise utilization of resources and protection of the natural environment. The conservation movement would be a parody without adequate emphasis on the wise utilization of the most precious of all resources—the irreplaceable human resources. The era of conservation has made an impact in the field of education, too, as indicated by attempts to efficiently deploy all human resources currently available in the schools to the end that all children may be provided with educationally sound and beneficial experiences. The era of conservation of human resources has set the stage for the appearance of the paraprofessional on the education scene.

ENTER THE PARAPROFESSIONAL

The new educational members have experienced a brief history marked by periods of rejection, periods of resistance, and periods of semi-acceptance by professional educators. Since the stormy 1956 beginnings, paraprofessionals have been employed in thousands of school systems within the United States with some remarkable and some disappointing results. Within the past decade, paraprofessional roles have evolved from such unproductive tasks as monitoring hallways and collecting monies to fulfilling roles which help to make education meaningful to children. The evolution of the paraprofessional roles also has been met with ambivalent feelings among professionals, particularly those who view their classrooms as inner sanctums. Recent developments, however, in the field of education such as increased school enrollments, pleas for accountability, implementation of new school organizational patterns, curricular revisions toward relevance, and demands for increased individualization of instruction have necessitated new roles for all participants in the educational drama.

Since neither time nor energy permits a single professional to fulfill the educational needs of all children with whom he may be entrusted while having to perform all the nonprofessional tasks which traditionally accompany teaching, the paraprofessional may provide the solution to several professional problems. It is through the paraprofessional that the professional's teaching talents may be released, that the "professional appendix" of nonprofessional duties may be severed from the role of the professional, and that the professional educator may be granted his "right to teach."

The paraprofessional may serve to enhance the role of the professional educator, freeing him to perform strictly professional functions. Because of the potential benefit which may accrue to children by including paraprofessionals in the classroom, educators must view paraprofessionals as valuable and vital members of the educational team. Unfortunately, such a viewpoint has not been present in many school systems. The lack of clearly defined roles and responsibilities of both professionals and paraprofessionals has contributed to the negative and ambivalent responses toward paraprofessionals. Many problems may be forestalled when roles and responsibilities are firmly established and clearly understood by all parties concerned. Paraprofessional duties should be determined through appraisal of educational experiences, special abilities, and areas of competence.

New Roles in Demand

Current practices in the use of paraprofessionals merely tap the surface of this potentially rich educational resource. Education which is relevant and personalized, as demanded by contemporary society, is an attainable goal only if schools utilize more effectively the available human resources. More effective utilization means that all professionals must assume new, more highly professional roles and that some paraprofessionals must assume more instructionally oriented roles, as dictated by their role descriptions and special competencies. Such practices as confining the duties of the paraprofessional to housekeeping chores remove him from the scene where his most valuable contribution may be made—in the classroom serving as a human resource to the learning processes of children.

Need for Effective Utilization of Personnel

Nowhere is the need for individualization of instruction more firmly established than in the reading program. The appalling statistics relative to number of nonreaders and underachievers in reading, number of school dropouts due to ineffective reading behaviors, and number of unemployables because of inability to read effectively clearly emphasize the need for wise use of resources, both human and material, in order to provide individualized instruction in reading.

Wise use of human resources, in this case, means the appropriate casting and the assigning to correct roles all participants in the reading program. The reading teacher and the paraprofessional must form an instructional team with complementary roles and with the common goal of enabling each student to become an independent reader inspired with a love of reading. The reading teacher must assume a leadership role in the team, supervising and guiding the paraprofessional. He must maintain responsibility for diagnosing reading strengths and weaknesses and prescribing learning experiences designed to enable students to develop reading skills.

ROLE OF THE PARAPROFESSIONAL IN THE READING PROGRAM

Paraprofessionals can perform functions which will aid teachers to be more effective in their teaching and teaching-related roles. Although paraprofessionals can assist in a variety of ways, the purpose of the remainder of this section is to propose a series of instruction-oriented tasks, some of which require paraprofessionals to have direct contact with children in a learning situation under the supervision of teachers. The tasks proposed are not intended to be exhaustive, but instead they are intended to stimulate reading teachers to think about the uses that can be made of paraprofessionals.

1. Paraprofessionals may apply readability formulas to books and materials in the classroom, thereby enabling teachers to help children select more appropriate books in terms of level of difficulty as well as interest level. Knowledge of the readability levels of books and materials may also enable teachers to make the necessary adjustments in teaching in the content areas other than reading. Paraprofessionals may also help children select books appropriate to their reading levels and interests.

2. Paraprofessionals can prepare teaching materials in reading such as specific word charts, vocabulary cards, phonic word wheels, sentence strips, and picture-word cards. They may also prepare teaching materials which motivate reading behaviors such as teaching games and devices. Research supports the fact that children learn through a variety of media; however, teachers' busy schedules make

SAM V. DAUZAT

it difficult for them to construct the multitude of devices which might make reading skills more easily attainable for children.

3. Paraprofessionals may reinforce specific reading skills through the implementation of a teaching game or drill exercise prescribed by the reading teacher. In the process of learning reading skills, children need many reinforcement activities. Those activities which require adult supervision may be directed by the paraprofessionals. It should be noted, however, that paraprofessionals must not be responsible for introducing new reading skills.

4. Under the supervision of the reading teacher, paraprofessionals can tutor children with special reading skills problems. Current research supports the fact that children make gains in reading ability under such programs. The paraprofessional, in this instance, should implement a teaching plan designed by the reading teacher and should not be expected to design teaching strategies independently.

5. Paraprofessionals may supervise children's independent work in reading, such as workbook activities or worksheet-type activities, and thereby free the teacher to give assistance to the other children.

6. Paraprofessionals can listen to the oral reading of children, perhaps even noting areas of consistent weaknesses for referral to the teacher of reading. It has long been recognized that children learn to refine reading skills by putting them into practice. The paraprofessional can provide the audience for purposeful oral reading particularly vital for remedial readers and disadvantaged children.

7. Paraprofessionals can extend the children's background of experiences by reading to them. Children must have words and concepts within their listening-meaning vocabularies, and perhaps within their speaking vocabularies, before they can be expected to read those words and concepts. Listening to stories read by an adult can contribute to children's growth in these areas.

8. Paraprofessionals can provide children with the suppor-

tive environment crucial to the development and maintenance of positive self-concepts which are intensely relevant to desirable reading behaviors. Paraprofessionals can increase each child's chance for personal attention and in so doing can help each child establish a more positive sense of worth. Effective reading behaviors flourish in such an environment.

9. Paraprofessionals can assist in the development of reading experience charts, both group and individual, to expand children's reading vocabularies through the graphic representation of their own experiences. Specific activities for paraprofessionals in this respect include a) recording children's dictated experiences, b) supervising children's illustrations for experience stories, and c) manuscripting or typing children's dictated sentences on reading experience charts.

10. Paraprofessionals can supervise small group dramatization of stories read by children. Children's oral reading skills and interpretive skills can be greatly enhanced by such activities, and paraprofessionals can be most effective in guiding them.

11. Paraprofessionals can supervise peer-tutoring in reading skills. Peer-tutoring holds great promise as an avenue for helping children extend reading skills, but it may require some adult supervision to minimize social disruptions which sometimes ensue.

12. Paraprofessionals can prepare instructional media designed to motivate recreational reading behaviors. Clever posters, bulletin boards, and book fairs may encourage recreational reading; and paraprofessionals can be key persons in the preparation and placement of such stimuli.

SUMMARY

Paraprofessionals have valuable roles to enact in the effective reading program. Use of paraprofessionals in the classroom, however, is justified only to the extent to which educational benefits accrue to the children in that classroom. Professionals must devise strategies whereby the resources in the classroom may be most effectively utilized and whereby the professional and paraprofessional may function as an educational team. Professionals must not squander the potential source of rich opportunities for children—the paraprofessional—on nonproductive tasks. Waste of natural resources is deplorable, but waste of human resources is intolerable. Thus, the professional teacher of reading must assume the key role while the paraprofessional assumes a supporting role, enhancing the opportunities of each to make a positive impact on the educational lives of children in the reading program.